Volume 6

make it yourself
The Complete Step-by-Step Library of Needlework and Crafts

COLUMBIA HOUSE/New York

Editor: Mary Harding
Assistant Editor: Margo Coughtrie
Editorial Assistants: Sally Fisher/Maureen Paton
Consultants: Greta Barrett/Angela Jeffs (Sewing)/
Patsy North (Embroidery and Crafts)/
Frances Rogers (Knitting and Crochet)
Managing Editor: Nicholas Wright
Design Co-ordinator: Jan Churcher
Production Control: Sheila Biddlecombe
Editorial Director: Graham Donaldson

© 1973/4/5/6 by Orbis-Verlag für Publizistik GMBH and Co. KG.
© 1975/6/7 Phoebus Publishing Company / BPC Publishing Ltd.

Distributed by Columbia House, 51 West 52nd Street, New York, New York 10019

Printed in U.S.A.

Introduction

Volume 6 of Make It Yourself is filled with an abundance of projects for creative minds and nimble fingers, as a quick glance through the pages will show you.

For knitting enthusiasts, there is a selection of fashionable patterns for all tastes, from a flattering cardigan with shaped bust darts to an up-to-the-minute pullover worked widthwise in garter stitch. For children, we feature sturdy knits for playtime as well as a lovable trio of sailor dolls.

Crochet addicts can get their hooks into a new technique—afghan crochet—which produces an attractive, firm fabric. Ever-popular Granny squares are given a new approach. Have you ever thought of working them in sisal for an original patchwork rug?

The dressmaking designs in this volume are chosen for all-season wear. There are raincoats for women and children, everyday skirts, sporty shirts for men and casual kimonos for the family. They are all very practical, but with those stylish touches that demand a second glance.

Modelling, painting, and printing feature in the crafts section. With very few materials, you can produce a set of puppets, paint on glass, or print with linoleum blocks. With such a wealth of ideas to inspire you, all you need to do is pick a project and begin creating.

make it yourself

Contents

		Page
How to use this book	Body measurements chart Fashion sizing Metric conversion Selecting a yarn	**648-649**
Knitting	How-to instructions Bolero Cardigans Dress Hats Jacket Playsuits Pullovers Scarves Stole Toys	**651-681**
Crochet	How-to instructions Afghans Bedspreads Cardigans Hats Pot holders Rug Scarves	**682-699**
Dressmaking	How-to instructions Jacket Raincoats Shirts Skirts	**700-715**
Sewing	Aprons Baby designs Bed caddy Jacket Kimonos Pullovers Skirts	**716-733**
Embroidery	How-to instructions Embroidery Patterns Patches Picture Small motifs Sports scenes	**734-749**
Crafts	How-to instructions Glass painting patterns Painting Printing Puppetmaking	**750-762**
Index		**763-764**
Notes		**765-768**

How to use this book..

Selecting a yarn

In this series, we are introducing a new and easy way to identify the yarn used in our knitting and crochet features! You will find an actual-size, colored photograph of the yarn given with each set of directions.

Materials Required:

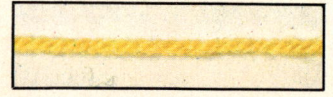

150 (200) gm or 6 (7) oz each of yellow and green, 50 gm or 2 oz blue [100 gm = 360 m or 390 yds]. Knitting needles size 4 (Am) or 10 (Eng).

At one time or another, you have probably suffered the disappointment of finding that the yarn specified in knitting and crochet directions is difficult to obtain or totally unavailable in your area. When this happens you are faced with the often impossible task of finding a substitute yarn. By matching a yarn against our photograph, you can choose a yarn of similar weight and texture from the range of yarns available in your store or favorite needlework shop.

This method is also helpful if you have yarn left over from other projects and you are unsure whether it is the proper weight or texture and whether you have sufficient yardage to finish a new shawl or pullover.

To help you determine the amount of yarn needed, we have also listed the yardage per skein for the yarn used. Most yarn companies give the yardage per skein in their sample books, and many shops have interchangeable yarn lists which give the yardages per unit weight. You will then be able to see whether you will need to make adjustments in the number of skeins required of the yarn which you have chosen.

Before you start to work the pattern, work a test swatch and match it against the Tension given in the directions (see the Tension Gauge instructions below). Adjust the needle or hook size if necessary. Any yarn which can be worked at the tension given in the directions can be used for that pattern.

Centimeters or inches?

The metric system of measurement is gaining greater use and acceptance, and some needlework and crafts equipment and materials are already sold by the metric weight and/or length. For your convenience, we have given all the weights and measures in both systems. <u>NOTE</u>: In some cases, the conversions are not exact. The measurements have been rounded to the nearest convenient or appropriate number.

Tension gauge

One key to successful knitting or crocheting is the tension! Each of our directions is based on the given tension gauge (number of rows and stitches to 10 cm or 4").

To check your tension, work a test piece 12 cm or 5" square in the stitch pattern. Make a cardboard template with a 10 cm or 4" square cut out of it. Place the template over your swatch and count the rows and stitches. Compare the numbers with the tension gauge given in the directions. If your swatch has too few stitches and rows, work more tightly or use smaller equipment. If you have more than the number given, use larger needles, or hook. Directions for the items shown can be used for any yarn of similar thickness and texture, providing you can achieve the proper tension.

Do not be upset if you find that you do have to adjust the needle or hook size. This does not mean that there is anything wrong with your knitting or crocheting. The needle and hook sizes given in the directions are an average, but by no means an absolute. There is great variation in the tension at which different people work, and you will even find slight variations in the tension of your work. On days when you are tense or tired, your knitting or crocheting will probably be a little tighter.

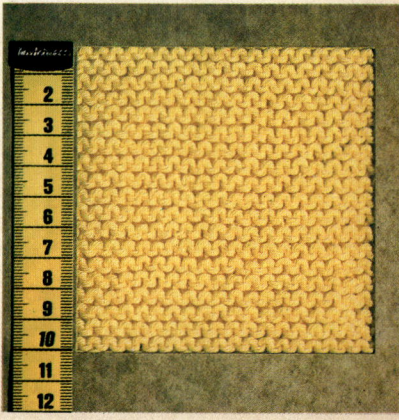

648

Fashion sizing

Dressmaking

Do you know your size? Don't just say 'yes', because as you already know, the fit of pattern and ready-to-wear sizes varies.

To eliminate confusion, we have lettered our sizes (A, B, C) instead of giving them the traditional numbering (10, 12).

Remeasure yourself and match your-body measurements with those given in the chart below. All of the patterns are designed according to these measurements, so choose the pattern size which is right for your measurements. You may have to make minor adjustments in the pattern pieces to adapt them to your body contours, and Dressmaking Pattern Sheet 2 explains how to do this. Other dressmaking pattern sheets will deal with more complex fitting for specific garments such as pants.

DO NOT MEASURE THE PATTERNS. Every pattern includes, according to the design, an added measure to allow for easy movement when wearing the garment. Just compare your body measurements with the measurements given in the chart and choose the proper size.

Each pattern is given in five sizes. Two of the sizes are given on the pattern sheet and the other three sizes can be easily drawn from the two sizes given. Directions for adapting for the three additional sizes are given on each pattern sheet. Even if you are not one of the standard pattern sizes, but are a mixed size made up of several standard measurements, you can still use our patterns. Since each pattern can be adapted for five sizes – a size smaller, a size larger, and a size between the two sizes actually marked on the pattern sheet – it is possible to construct a pattern for yourself. Directions for constructing a mixed-size pattern are given on Dressmaking Pattern Sheet 2.

Knitting and Crochet

The knitting and crochet sizes are based on the Dressmaking Body Measurements Chart. For each direction, you will be given the actual body measurements for which the garment is intended. The finished knitted or crocheted garment will be larger than the given measurements to allow for comfort and movement.

Size: Directions are for 92 cm (36″) bust. Changes for 96, 100 cm (37½″, 39½″) bust are in brackets.

Do you know your size?

Don't just say 'yes'. Remeasure yourself, following the diagrams and instructions, and then check the Body Measurements chart.

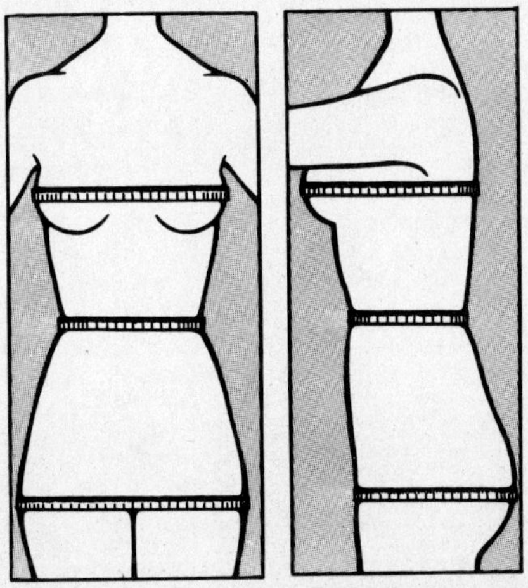

Bust – measure around the fullest part of the bust.

Waist – tie a string around your body so that it settles comfortably at your natural waistline. Measure your waist at the string.

Hips – measure around the fullest part of your hips (this generally falls 7″–9″ below your waistline).

Important hints:

When taking measurements, do not hold the tape measure slack or pull it too tight. The tape must lie evenly horizontal all around the body – it should not go up at the back and down at the front. You will find it simpler and more accurate to be measured by someone else.

Body measurements chart

WOMEN

Size	A	B	C	D	E	F	G	H
Bust	80 cm (31½″)	84 cm (33″)	88 cm (34½″)	92 cm (36″)	96 cm (37½″)	100 cm (39½″)	104 cm (41″)	108 cm (42½″)
Waist	59 cm (23¼″)	63.5 cm (25″)	68 cm (26½″)	72.5 cm (28½″)	77 cm (30½″)	81.5 cm (32″)	86 cm (34″)	90 cm (35½″)
Hips	86 cm (34″)	90 cm (35½″)	94 cm (37″)	98 cm (38½″)	102 cm (40″)	106 cm (42″)	110 cm (43½″)	114 cm (45″)

MEN

Size	J	K	L	M	N	O	P	Q
Chest	84 cm (33″)	88 cm (34½″)	92 cm (36″)	96 cm (37½″)	100 cm (39½″)	104 cm (41″)	108 cm (42½″)	112 cm (44″)
Hip	88 cm (34½″)	92 cm (36″)	96 cm (37½″)	100 cm (39½″)	104 cm (41″)	108 cm (42½″)	112 cm (44″)	116 cm (45½″)
Neck	36 cm (14″)	37 cm (14½″)	38 cm (15″)	39 cm (15½″)	40 cm (15¾″)	41 cm (16″)	42 cm (16½″)	43 cm (17″)
Arm	60 cm (23¾″)	61 cm (24″)	62 cm (24¼″)	63 cm (24¾″)	64 cm (25¼″)	65 cm (25½″)	66 cm (26″)	67 cm (26½″)

CHILDREN

Size	S	T	U	V	W	X	Y	Z
Height	110 cm (43″)	116 cm (45½″)	122 cm (48″)	128 cm (50½″)	134 cm (52¾″)	140 cm (55″)	146 cm (57½″)	152 cm (60″)
Chest	60 cm (23¾″)	62 cm (24¼″)	64 cm (25¼″)	66 cm (26″)	68 cm (26¾″)	70 cm (27½″)	73 cm (28¾″)	76 cm (29¾″)
Waist	58 cm (23″)	59 cm (23¼″)	60 cm (23¾″)	61 cm (24″)	62 cm (24¼″)	63 cm (24¾″)	64 cm (25¼″)	65 cm (25¾″)
Hips	66 cm (26″)	68 cm (26¾″)	70 cm (27½″)	72 cm (28¼″)	74 cm (29″)	76 cm (29¾″)	80 cm (31½″)	84 cm (33″)

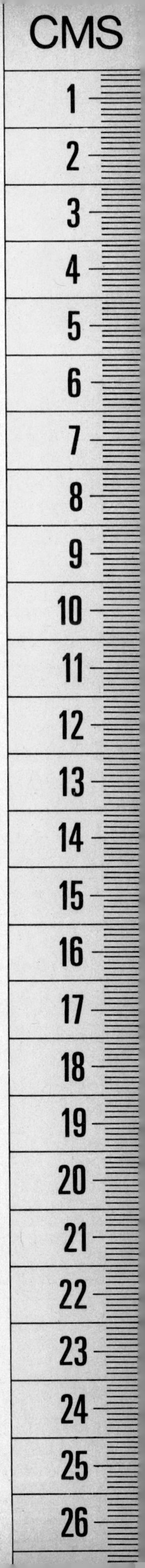

Knitting

A layer of luxury

The perfect cover-up! Loungers will love this roomy stole in soft mohair. With its delicate color mixture and long fringes, it will slip like a dream over any outfit.

STOLE

Size: 200 cm x 80 cm or 79" x 31".
Materials Required:

560 gm or 20 oz of blended mixture or plain mohair [40 gm = 64 m or 70 yds]. Knitting needles size 10 (Am) or 4 (Eng).
Basic Stitch: St st.
Tension: 14 sts and 18 R = 10 cm or 4".
Abbreviations: K = knit. P = purl. St(s) = stitch(es). R = row(s). St st = stocking or stockinette stitch.

DIRECTIONS
Cast on 110 sts; work in st st for 200 cm or 79". Cast off loosely. Cut 35 cm or 14" strands and knot fringe along short edges.

MOHAIR JACKET

Sizes: Directions are for 92 cm or 36" bust. Changes for 100 cm or 39½" bust are in brackets.
Materials Required: Yarn: (see Stole sample) 440 (480) gm or 16 (17) oz blended mixture or plain mohair. Knitting needles size 8 (Am) or 6 (Eng). St holders.
Basic Stitch and Abbreviations: See Stole.
Tension: 15 sts and 22 R = 10 cm or 4".

DIRECTIONS
Back: Cast on 80 (86) sts and work 4 R in K 1, P 1 rib, then continue in st st decreasing 1 st at both ends of every 24th R 3 times — 74 (80) sts. Work straight to 45 (46) cm or 17½" (18"). Cast off.
Left Front: Cast on 38 (41) sts and work 4 R in K 1, P 1 rib, then continue in st st, decreasing 1 st at right edge as on Back — 35 (38) sts. Cast off at 45 (46) cm or 17½" (18").
Right Front: As for Left Front, reversing shapings.
Sleeves and Yokes: Begin at cuff of left sleeve. Cast on 74 sts and work 4 R in K 1, P 1 rib. Work in st st to 58 (60) cm or 22¾" (23½"), ending after a P R.
Divide for Neck: K 37 sts, turn and place unworked 37 sts for Left Front on st holder. Continue on first sts for Back, and at neck edge, in every 2nd R cast off 2 sts 1 time and 1 st 2 times — 33 sts.
Work straight to 75 (77) cm or 29½" (30¼"). At neck edge, in every 2nd R increase 1 st 2 times, then cast on 2 sts 1 time and end at neck edge. Place the 37 sts on st holder.
Go back to Left Front sts and at beginning of every K row, cast off 4 sts 8 times and 5 sts 1 time. For Right Front, cast on 5 sts, P 1 R, then at beginning of every K R cast on 4 sts 8 times — 37 sts. P next R then P across 37 Back sts. Continue in st st on the 74 sts to 134 (138) cm or 53¾" (54¼"). Work 4 R in K 1, P 1 rib. Cast off.
Finishing: Steam lightly on wrong side. Join seams, joining lower 15 cm or 6" of Sleeves from right side for turn-back of cuff. With right side facing, pick up and K 68 (70) sts from straight part of Fronts, 40 sts along Front slopes, and 35 sts from Back neck edge. Work 7 cm or 2¾" in K 1, P 1 rib. Cast off in rib. Turn band to right side for 5 cm or 2" and sew down.

The long loose jacket is knitted in the same yarn as the stole. It is shaped like a kimono jacket, with wide sleeves and no fastenings for maximum versatility. The front band is sewn on.

► Here you can see the back of the jacket. The sleeves and yoke are knitted in one piece across the back.

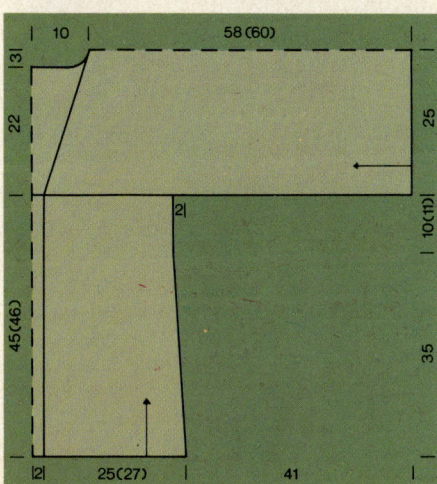

◄ Half-pattern for small (large) size. The pieces are knitted in the direction of the arrows. Numbers are centimeters; inches are in the directions.

Knitting

Cardigan in large sizes

Slimming lines

This long-line cardigan has a flattering effect on all figures. The vertical line of the edged borders will make you appear taller and the darts and fitted waist shape the cardigan to the contours of your body.

Knitting

Bust darts are knitted into the piece to shape the fronts so that they will lie close to the body.

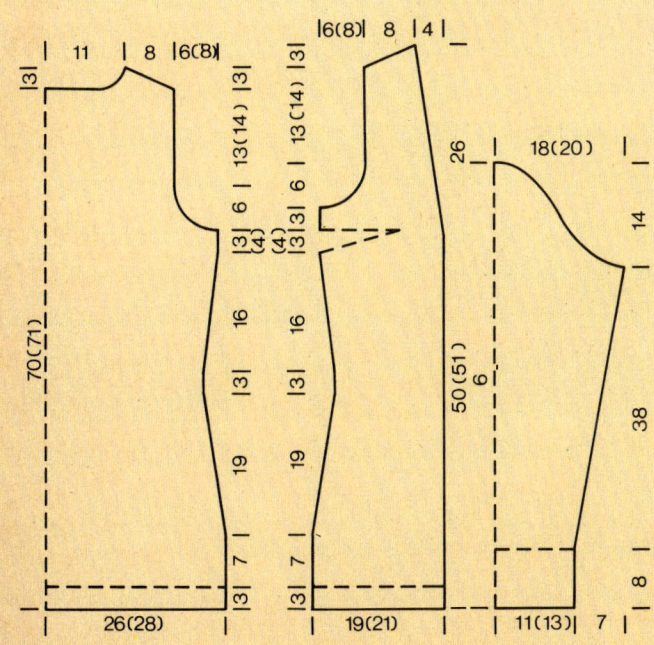

Half-patterns for the smallest (largest) sizes. Measurements are in centimeters; inch equivalents are in the directions.

Size: Directions are for 100 cm or 39½" bust. Changes for 104 (108) cm or 41" (42½") bust are in brackets.

Materials Required:

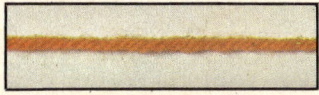

500 (550:550) gm or 18 (20:20) oz grey, 50 gm or 2 oz white [50 gm = 210 m or 230 yds]. Knitting needles and a circular needle size 2 (Am) or 11 (Eng). Stitch holder.

Basic Pattern: Stocking or stockinette stitch.

Tension: 28 sts and 40 R = 10 cm or 4".

Abbreviations: St(s) = stitch(es). R = row(s). K = knit. P = purl. St st = stocking or stockinette stitch.

DIRECTIONS

Back: With grey, cast on 146 (152:158) sts and work in st st for 3 cm or 1", ending after a purl R. P next R for hem fold line. Beginning with a P R, continue in st st, decreasing 1 st at each end of next R, then every 10th R 7 times more — 130 (136:142) sts. Work straight to 32 cm or 12½", then increase 1 st each end of next R and every 12th R 5 times more — 142 (148: 154) sts. Work to 51 cm or 20".

Shape Armholes: Cast off 3 sts at beginning of next 4 R, 2 sts at beginning of next 4 R, 1 st at beginning of next 10 R, then 1 st each end of every 4th R 2 times. For 2nd and 3rd sizes only, decrease 1 st each end of every 8th R 3 (6) times. For all sizes, continue straight on 108 sts to 70 (70.5:71) cm or 27½" (27¾":28").

Shape Shoulders and Neck: Cast off center 46 sts and work each side separately. Decrease 3 sts at the beginning of next 2 neck edge R, then 1 st on next 2 neck edge R. *At the same time,* at armhole edge, cast off 3 sts 1 time and 4 sts 5 times.

Right Front: With grey, cast on 53 (56:59) sts. Shape side, armhole, and shoulder to match Back. *At the same time,* at 48 cm or 19", shape bustline: K to last 5 (4:4) sts, turn the piece. Increase 1 st by passing the yarn around the needle, K to the end. Continue thus, leaving 5 (4: 4) more sts at the end of each side edge R 3 (5:5) times and 5 (4:5) sts 2 times, increasing 1 st each time for turning. In the next R, work across all sts, working each increased st together with st next to it. *At the same time,* at 50 (51:51) cm or 19¾" (20": 20") decrease 1 st at Front edge on next R, then every 6th R 12 times more.

Left Front: Work to match Right Front, reversing all shapings.

Sleeves: Cast on 62 (68: 72) sts and work in K 1, P 1 rib for 7 cm or 2¾". Join white and work 4 R in rib. Break off white. Change to grey and work in st st, increasing 1 st each end alternately on every 6th and 8th R 20 times — 102 (108: 112) sts. Continue straight to 46 cm or 18".

Shape Top: Cast off 3 (4:4) sts at beginning of next 4 R, 2 sts on next 12 R, 1 st at beginning of next 24 R, 2 sts on next 12 R and 3 (3: 4) sts on next 4 R. Cast off remaining 6 (8:8) sts.

Border: With white, cast 551 (555:557) sts onto the circular needle and work back and forth in K 1, P 1 rib for 3 R. Change to grey and work for 8 cm or 3¼". Cast off.

Finishing: Press work lightly. Join seams, then turn hem to wrong side and slip-stitch in place. Sew border to front and neck edges along the cast-on edge of the border. Sew the border with even backstitch worked in white yarn on the right side of the piece.

655

Bust darts, Sewing on a border

How-to

Making a bust dart

1 On the knit side, leave the required number of stitches unworked; turn piece. Pass yarn around right needle; work the stitches on left needle.

2 On the purl side, leave the required number of stitches unworked; turn piece. Pass yarn around right needle; work the stitches on left needle.

3 When the bottom half of the knit-side dart has been completed, work across all of the stitches held on the left needle, working each increased stitch together with the following stitch in a twisted knit stitch.

4 When the bottom half of the purl-side dart has been completed, work across all of the stitches held on the left needle, working each increased stitch together with the following stitch in a twisted purl stitch.

Sewing on a border

1 To join an edging onto a piece, baste the cast-on or cast-off edge onto the right side of the piece.

2 Sew the border on with even backstitches worked on the right side of the piece.

Knitting in two colors
A country classic

Knitting

This is a country-girl look you can wear anywhere. The tweed-like pattern is worked with two shades of green.

Knitting

Size: Directions are for 88 cm or 34½" bust. Changes for 96 cm or 37½" bust are in brackets.

Materials Required:

210 (240) gm or 8 (9) oz dark green, 180 gm or 7 oz light green. Knitting needles and a circular needle size 2 (Am) or 11 (Eng).

Basic Pattern: R 1: *K 1 light green, K 1 dark green, repeat from * to end. R 2: *P 1 dark green, P 1 light green, repeat from * to end. These 2 R form the repeat.

Border Pattern: K 1, P 1 rib.

Tension: 32 sts and 32 R = 10 cm or 4".

Abbreviations: St(s) = stitch(es). K = knit. P = purl. R = row(s). Rnd(s) = round(s).

DIRECTIONS

Back: Using dark green, cast on 126 (140) sts and work 14 cm or 5½" in Border Pattern, increasing 20 sts evenly across last R – 146 (160) sts. Change to Basic Pattern and work straight to 39 cm or 15½".

Shape Armholes: Cast off 3 sts at beginning of next 4 (6) R, 2 sts at beginning of next 8 R, and 1 st at beginning of next 10 R – 108 (116) sts. Work straight to 56 (57) cm or 22" (22½").

Shape Neck and Shoulders: Cast off center 44 sts and work on each side separately. At the neck edge, on every 2nd R cast off 2 sts 2 times, then 1 st 2 times. *At the same time,* at 57 (58) cm or 22½" (23"), cast off 8 (10) sts at beginning of next armhole edge R and 9 (10) sts at beginning of next 2 armhole edge R.

Front: Work as for Back to 35 (36) cm or 13¾" (14¼").

Divide for Neck: Work across 73 (80) sts, turn, and work on each side separately. At neck edge, on every 2nd R cast off 2 sts 5 times, 1 st 10 times, then decrease 1 st every 4th R 8 times. *At the same time,* shape armhole to match Back, and when piece measures 40 cm or 15¾", begin stripe pattern. Work in stripes of 6 R dark green in stocking or stockinette st, then 10 R in the Basic Pattern. At 57 (58) cm or 22½" (23") shape shoulder to match Back.

Sleeves: Using dark green, cast on 70 (76) sts and work 16 cm or 6¼" in Border Pattern, increasing 14 sts evenly on last R – 84 (90) sts. Change to Basic Pattern and increase 1 st each end on every 8th and 10th R alternately 12 times – 108 (114) sts. Continue straight to 53 cm or 21".

Shape Top: Cast off 3 sts at beginning of next 6 R, 2 sts at beginning of next 32 (34) R, then 3 sts at beginning of next 4 R. Cast off remaining 14 (16) sts.

Neckband: Using circular needle and dark green, cast on 246 sts and mark a st for V point, then K in rnds. In every 3rd rnd, decrease for V-neck by slipping marked st and st to right of it, K next st and pass the 2 slipped sts over. Rib for 4 cm or 1½". Cast off in rib.

Finishing: Press with a warm iron over damp cloth. Join seams, sewing seam on right side for turn-back of cuffs. Sew neckband to neck edge. Press seams.

There are four plain-colored stripes across the front to add a distinctive touch to the simple style.

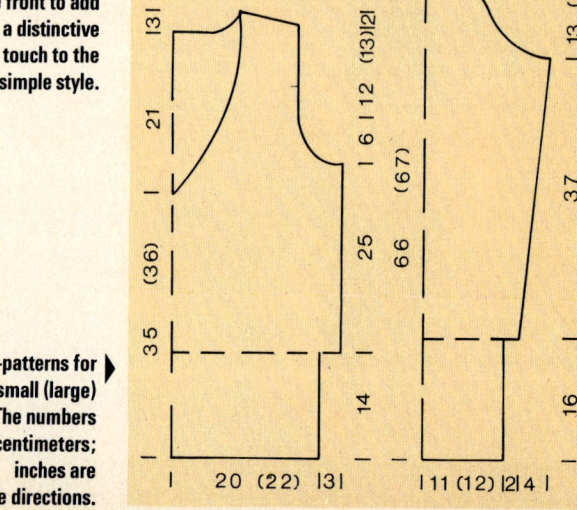

Half-patterns for the small (large) size. The numbers are centimeters; inches are in the directions.

Knitting in two colors

With crossed strands over your forefinger

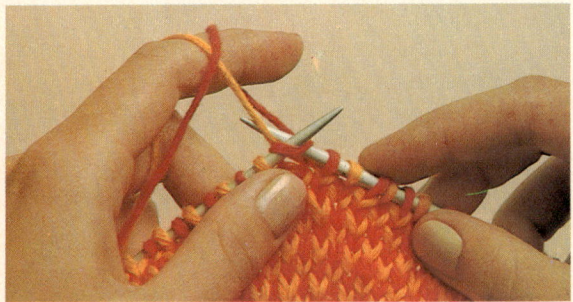
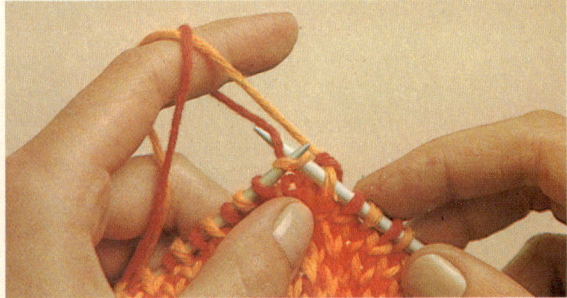

1 Cross the two colors over your forefinger so that one lies over the top from front to back and the other is passed under and over from back to front. Grasp the strands in your palm.

2 Knit as usual, working with one strand and then the other as the color pattern requires. The strand not in use is carried loosely along behind the piece. Work in a practice piece to check tension.

With two fingers

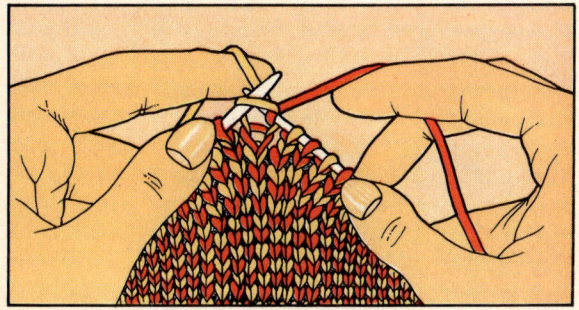
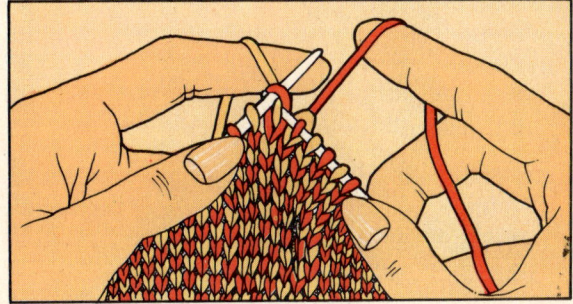

1 Place one color over the forefinger of your right hand and the other over the forefinger of your left hand. With the color held in your right hand, knit in the usual way.

2 To knit with the color held in your left hand, insert the needle into the stitch, pass the yarn over the needle from front to back, and draw the yarn through the stitch.

Spanning large color areas

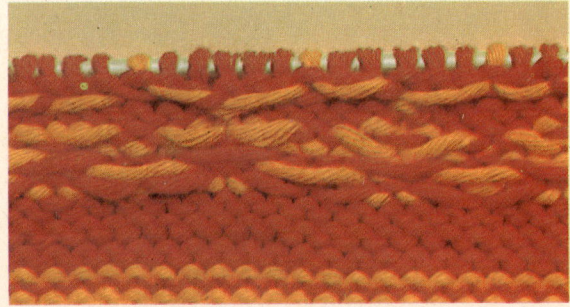

1 When the pattern requires you to carry a strand across a large color area, occasionally twist the carried strand together with the working strand.

2 The twisting of the strands will make shorter loops on the wrong side of the piece. This means that the loops will be less likely to catch in wear.

Random-colored yarn used double will make the patterning of your sweater and hat set unique! The pullover is a simple shape worked in garter stitch, making it a good project for beginners. The pullover is worked from front to back in one piece, then the collar piece is sewn on.

All shades of the rainbow

Size: Directions are for 88 cm or 34½" bust. Changes for 96 cm or 37½" bust are in brackets.

Materials Required:

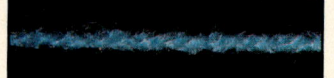

Pullover: 750 (800) gm or 27 (29) oz random-colored yarn. Hat: 150 gm or 6 oz random-colored yarn. [50 gm = 140 m or 150 yds]. Knitting needles size 8 (Am) or 6 (Eng).

Basic Stitch: Garter st.

Tension: 15 sts and 29 R = 10 cm or 4" with yarn used double.

Abbreviations: K = knit. P = purl. St(s) = stitch(es). R = row(s).

PULLOVER

This is worked in one piece, with exception of collar. Begin at Front and with yarn used double, cast on 74 (80) sts and work in Basic Pattern, decreasing 1 st each end of every 32nd R 3 times — 68 (74) sts. Work straight to 45 cm or 17½", noting how many R you have worked straight.

Shape Sleeves: At beginning of next 2 R, cast on 57 sts and continue straight on the 182 (188) sts to 48 cm or 19".

Shape Neck: Cast off center 26 sts, and work on each set of 78 (81) sts separately to 69 cm or 27", then cast on 26 sts at center and K across all sts 1 more time — 182 (188) sts. Work straight to 85 cm or 33½".

Shape Sleeves: At beginning of next 2 R, cast off 57 sts and continue on the 68 (74) sts for same number of R as worked straight on Front. Now increase 1 st each end of next R and every 32nd R 2 times more — 74 (80) sts. Work straight to 130 cm or 51" and cast off on a wrong side R.

Collar: Using yarn double, cast on 33 sts and work in K 1, P 1 rib for 64 cm or 25". Cast off in rib.

Finishing: Join seam, sewing the lower 10 cm or 4" of sleeve from right side for turn-back of cuff. Sew in Collar, sewing the cast-on edge under Front neck edge neatly. Sew remainder around neck edge, sewing cast-off edge behind cast-on edge. Turn over Collar as shown and turn back cuffs.

HAT

Using yarn double, cast on 27 sts for brim and work in garter st for 50 cm or 19½". Cast off. Using a flat seam, join cast-on and cast-off edges together. For the crown, using yarn double, cast on 78 sts and work in garter st for 12 cm or 4¾". Decrease in next R thus: *K 7, K 2 together, K 8, K 2 together, repeat from *, ending K 2 — 70 sts. Decrease thus on every 2nd R 7 times more, but work 1 st less between decreases each time — 14 sts remain. Cut yarn and draw through the 14 sts and fasten off.

Finishing: Join seam of crown, then sew on brim with seam to right side. Turn back brim.

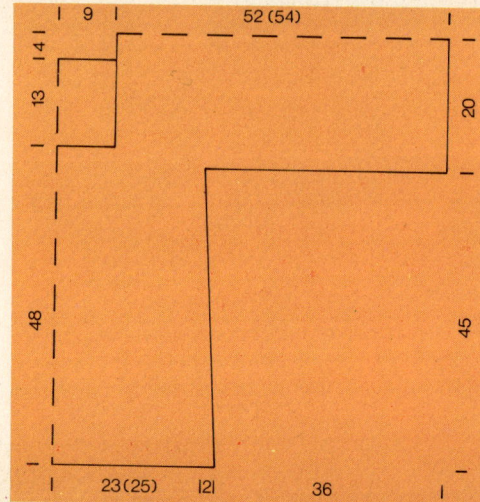

The sweater has wide kimono sleeves and is knitted in one piece in simple garter stitch. The pull-on hat is knitted in the same stitch.

Half-pattern for small (large) size. Numbers are centimeters; inches are in the directions.

Easy pattern in garter stitch

Simple to make and simple to wear

This easy-to-knit style is worked in one piece, from one sleeve across to the other. It is so roomy and comfortable, that you will want to wear it with everything from dresses to roll necks to shirts.

Size: Directions are for 88 cm or 34½" bust. Changes for 96 cm or 37½" bust are in brackets.

Materials Required:

700 (800) gm or 25 (29) oz orange or blue. [100 gm = 87 m or 95 yds]. Knitting needles size 10½ (Am) or 2 (Eng). Crochet hook F (Am) or 4.00 (Eng). St holder.

Basic Pattern: Garter st (K every R).

Tension: 12 sts and 24 R = 10 cm or 4".

Abbreviations: K = knit. St(s) = stitch(es). R = row(s).

DIRECTIONS

Note: The entire sweater is worked in one piece from side to side. Begin at left sleeve edge. Cast on 48 (50) sts. Work straight in garter st to 35 cm or 13¾".

Shape Armholes: At beginning of every R, cast on 1 st 10 times and 2 sts 2 times. At beginning of next 2 R cast on 35 sts for Back and Front — 132 (134) sts.

Work straight to 49 (50) cm or 19¼" (19½").

Divide for Back and Front: For Back, work over 66 (67) sts, turn and work straight on these sts for 26 (28) cm or 10¼" (11") ending at neck edge. Place sts on st holder. Go back to other 66 (67) sts. Begin at neck edge and decrease 1 st, then at same edge decrease 1 st alternately in every 4th and 6th R 5 times — 60 (61) sts. Work straight for 6 cm or 2½". Work in reverse by increasing 1 st at neck edge on next R, then every 4th and 6th R alternately 5 times — 66 (67) sts.

Now K across all 132 (136) sts. Work straight to 83 (87) cm or 33" (34½"). At beginning of R, cast off 35 sts 2 times, 2 sts 2 times, and 1 st 10 times — 48 (50) sts. Work straight for 35 cm or 13¾". Cast off.

Finishing: Join side and sleeve seams, sewing seam on right side for 15 cm or 6" at lower edge of sleeve to allow for turn-back. Using crochet hook, work slip stitches around neck to give a neat edge.

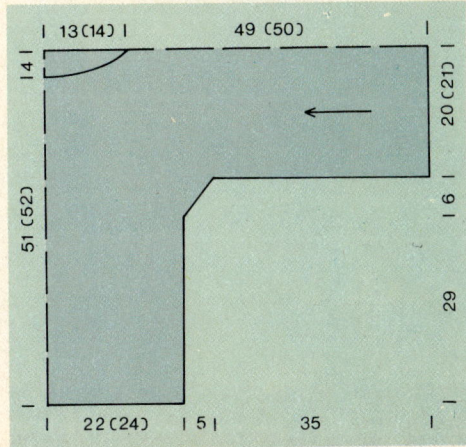

▲ The garter stitch pattern worked on large needles makes quick work of this pullover.

◄ Half-pattern for small (large) size. Numbers are centimeters; inches are given in the directions.

663

Size: Directions are for 84 cm or 33″ bust. Changes for 92 cm or 36″ bust are in brackets.
Materials Required:

Cardigan: 550 (600) gm or 20 (22) oz white. Bolero: 350 (400) gm or 13 (15) oz brown. Knitting needles size 7 (Am and Eng).
Basic Pattern: Stocking or stockinette st.
Tension: 15 sts and 26 R = 10 cm or 4″.
Abbreviations: P = purl. St(s) = stitch(es). R = row(s).

SLEEVELESS CARDIGAN

Back: Cast on 72 (78) sts and work in Basic Pattern, decreasing 1 st each end of every 30th R 3 times — 66 (72) sts. **Work straight for 20 (21) cm or 8″ (8¼″).
Shape Armholes: At beginning of every R, cast off 2 sts 6 times and 1 st 4 times — 50 (56) sts. Work straight for 5 (6) cm or 2 (2¼″), * then increase 1 st at each end of every 2nd R 2 times, cast on 2 sts at beginning of next 2 R, repeat from * 1 time more, then increase 1 st each end of next 2nd R — 68 (74) sts. Work straight to 69 (71) cm or 27¼″ (28″).
Shape Shoulders: At beginning of every R, cast off 1 st 4 times, 2 sts 6 times, then 4 (5) sts 2 (4) times, 5 (6) sts 4 (2) times. *At the same time,* at 73 (75) cm or 28¾″ (29½″), cast off center 16 (18) sts and work on each side separately, casting off 2 sts at neck edge on 2nd R 2 times.
Left Front: Cast on 36 (39) sts and work in Basic Pattern, shaping side, armhole, and shoulder as for Back. *At the same time,* at 65 (67) cm or 25½″ (26½″), shape neck by casting off at beginning of every P R 4 sts 1 time, 3 sts 1 time, 2 sts 1 time, and 1 st 3 (4) times.
Right Front: Work to match Left Front, reversing all shapings.
Pockets: Cast on 28 (30) sts and work to 24 (25) cm or 9½″ (9¾″). Cast off.
Finishing: Using a 4-ply yarn, sew up seams. Sew on pockets 3 cm or 1¼″ from lower edge.

BOLERO

Back: Cast on 66 (72) sts and work in Basic Pattern from ** of Cardigan. Work armhole, shoulder, and neck as for Cardigan, allowing for length difference (see pattern).
Left Front: Cast on 33 (36) sts and shape armhole and shoulder as for Back, shaping neck at 30 (32) cm or 11¾″ (12¼″) to match Cardigan.
Right Front: Work to match Left Front, reversing shapings.
Finishing: Using a 4-ply yarn, sew up seams.

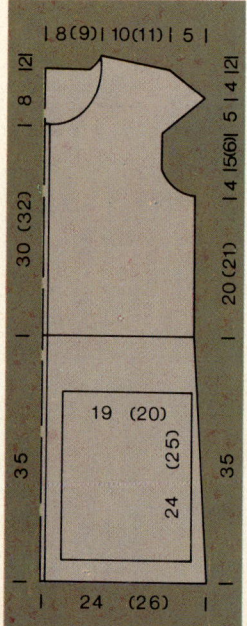

▲ Half-pattern in small (large) size for the bolero and sleeveless cardigan. Numbers are centimeters; inches are given in the directions. Bolero length is marked by horizontal line.

Wild and woolly fashions

Here are two styles to make in a soft looped wool: one short, the other long. Both are knitted without fastenings or borders and the long style has patch pockets.

664

Scarf style

Wrap yourself up in a luxury fringed scarf that is light enough to team with a special suit or dress and snug enough to wear on a cold day with a coat or cape.

FOR BOTH SCARVES

Materials Required:

[50 gm = 145 m or 158 yds]. See individual directions for colors and quantities of yarn.
Circular knitting needle size 2 (Am) or 11 (Eng).
Basic Stitch: Garter st (K every R).
Tension: 24 sts and 56 R = 10 cm or 4".
Abbreviations: K = knit. St(s) = stitch(es). R = row(s).

BLUE STRIPES

Size: 180 cm or 71" long and 17.5 cm or 7" wide.
Yarn: 50 gm or 4 oz each of blue, pink, turquoise, and brown.
Color Sequence: Cast on in blue, then 3 R blue; *4 R pink; 2 R each turquoise, brown, blue, and pink; 4 R each turquoise and brown; 2 R each blue, pink, turquoise and brown; 4 R blue; repeat from *.

DIRECTIONS

Using blue, cast on 438 sts for whole length and work back and forth in Basic Stitch, following the Color Sequence and repeating the 32 R 3 times. Cast off in the last blue R using a larger needle to avoid a tight edge.
Finishing: For fringe, cut 40 cm or 15½" lengths, and using 3 strands of the appropriate color, knot into the edge, but when working over the 2-R stripes use 2 lengths of one color and one of another to match row ends.

BROWN STRIPES

Size: 180 cm or 71" long, and 13.75 cm or 5¼" wide.
Yarn: 50 gm or 2 oz each of brown, pink, and beige.
Color Sequence: Cast on in brown, then 1 R brown, *2 R each pink, brown, pink, brown, beige, brown, beige, brown, repeat from *.

DIRECTIONS

Using brown, cast on 438 sts for whole length and work back and forth in Basic Stitch, following the Color Sequence and repeating the 16 R from * 4 times. Work another 2 R each of pink, brown, pink, then 1 R brown and cast off in brown using a larger size needle.
Finishing: For fringe, cut 40 cm or 15½" lengths and using 3 at a time, knot into edge in appropriate colors.

Here is a color variation using subtle tones that blend to give an interesting effect.

Knitting

Bright red and dazzling white have strong fluorescent qualities, yet will still harmonize well with winter clothes.

Clever coloring for safety

Safety first!

Many of the colors in yarns, particularly Orlon, have an almost fluorescent quality. You will find that they are perfect for making hats and scarves that are not only warm, but will keep a child safe on dark winter days.

ALL DESIGNS
Materials Required:

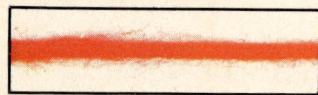

Amounts and colors are in the individual directions. Knitting needles size 2 (Am) or 10 (Eng).
Basic Stitch: K 1, P 1 rib.
Tension: Hat: 22 sts and 33 R (slightly stretched) = 10 cm or 4". Scarf: 25 sts and 32 R (unstretched) = 10 cm or 4".
Abbreviations: K = knit. P = purl. St(s) = stitch(es). R = row(s).

DESIGN A
Materials Required: Yarn: Hat: 30 gm or 1½ oz red and 20 gm or 1 oz each of blue and white. Scarf: 70 gm or 3 oz red and 20 gm or 1 oz each of blue and white.

DIRECTIONS
Hat: Using red, cast on 106 sts and work in Basic Stitch for 13 cm or 5", then work 8 R in each of white, blue, red, white, blue. Continue in red decreasing thus: R 1: * Rib 2, slip 1, K 1, pass slip st over, repeat from * ending K 1, P 1 – 80 sts. R 2 and all even numbered R: Work in rib, allowing for decreased sts. R 3: * Rib 1, slip 1, K 1, pass slipped st over, repeat from * to end, Rib 2 – 54 sts. R 5: *Rib 4, slip 1, K 1, pass slipped st over, repeat from * to end – 45 sts. R 7: *Rib 3, slip 1, K 1, pass slipped st over, repeat from * to end – 36 sts. R 9: *Rib 2, slip 1, K 1, pass slipped st over, repeat from * to end – 27 sts. R 11: *Rib 1, slip 1, K 1, pass slipped st over, repeat from * to end – 18 sts. R 13: Work 2 together to end – 9 sts. Break yarn, and thread through the 9 sts, draw up and sew back

On the two sets of hats and scarves shown here the predominantly fluorescent color is yellow. Not only is it cheerful and sunny, but it also looks good with all other colors.

seam, sewing the lower 9 cm or 3½" on right side. **Scarf:** Using red, cast on 43 sts and work in Basic Stitch for 100 cm or 39" and work 8 R each in red, white, blue, repeat from * once, work in red for 70 cm or 27½", then repeat the stripe in reverse order. Work a knotted fringe into each short edge.

DESIGN B
Materials Required: Yarn: Hat: 20 gm or 1 oz each in green, yellow, and red. Scarf: 40 gm or 2 oz green and red and 30 gm or 1½ oz yellow.

DIRECTIONS
<u>Hat:</u> Work as for Design A, but cast on in green and work 12 cm or 4¾", then work (6 R yellow, 6 R red) 3 times, 6 R yellow. Work the decreases for crown in red.
<u>Scarf:</u> Work as for Design A, working in color sequence of * (6 R red, 6 R yellow) 2 times, 6 R red, 20 R green, repeat from * 6 times, then work red and yellow stripes to match beginning.

DESIGN C
Materials Required: Yarn: <u>Hat:</u> 20 gm or 1 oz each of red and yellow, 10 gm or ½ oz blue. <u>Scarf:</u> 30 gm or 1½ oz each blue and yellow. 60 gm or 2½ oz red.

DIRECTIONS
<u>Hat:</u> Work as for Design A, but cast on in red and work 11 cm or 4¼", then work 16 R blue and (8 R yellow, 8 R red) 2 times. Work head decreases in yellow.
<u>Scarf:</u> Work as for Design A, working in color sequence of *8 R red, 8 R yellow, 16 R blue, repeat from * to desired length, ending with 8 R yellow to balance the stripe pattern.

669

Ship ahoy!

Use up your remnants of yarn to knit these brightly-colored jolly sailors for the family.

FOR ALL STYLES
Height: 25 cm or 10".
Materials Required:

[50 gm = 100 m or 109 yds]. Colors and quantities are given in individual directions. Knitting needles size 5 (Am) or 8 (Eng). Kapok. Felt: Small amounts red and black.
Basic Stitch: St st.
Tension: 18 sts and 26 R = 10 cm or 4".
Abbreviations: K = knit. P = purl. St(s) = stitch(es). St st = stocking or stockinette stitch. R = row(s).

JIM
Additional Materials: Yarn: Remnants of blue, grey, white, black, and red. 4 gold buttons. Red pompon.

DIRECTIONS
Legs: (make 2) Cast on 24 sts in black and work 2 cm or ¾" for feet in st st, then work 6 cm or 2½" in grey.
Body: Work across the 2 legs in blue and continue in st st for 10 cm or 4".
Head: Work 8 R white, 2 R blue, K 2 R white, then continue in blue st st to 25 cm or 10" from beginning. Cast off.
Arms: (make 2) Using white, cast on 12 sts and work 6 R in st st. Work left arm in blue to 12 cm or 4¾". Cast off. For right arm, work 2 R blue in st st and 2 R white in garter st alternately 3 times, then work in blue st st to 12 cm or 4¾". Cast off.

Finishing: Fold piece to form a back seam, then join leg and back seams. Stuff to a nice shape. Stitch across feet, legs, and neck. Join top head seam. Stuff and sew up arms slanting the cast-on edge, then sew to body as shown. Sew a red pompon to top of head. Using white, embroider the front inset with duplicate stitch or Swiss darning. Sew on felt eyes, cheeks, and tie. Embroider mouth and rank on arms. Sew on buttons.

JOHNNY
Additional Materials: Yarn: 50 gm or 2 oz white, remnants of black, red, and blue. 6 black buttons. St holders.

Legs and Body: Work as for Jim, but with feet in black and remainder in white. Continue across all sts to 9 cm or 3½", ending after a P R. In next R K 15 sts, leave next 18 sts on st holder, cast on 18 sts, K 15 sts. Continue in st st to 15 cm or 6", ending after a P R. Go back to center 18 sts and work in st st to 15 cm or 6" from beginning, keeping 2 sts each end in garter st, ending after a P R. Place in front of main piece and work across, knitting together 1 st from each set in center. Work straight, but at center front, work 2 sts in garter st on next R, then on every 2nd R work 1 st more in garter

670

st either side until body is completed as for Jim.

Head: Work in white as for Jim.

Arms: (make 2) Using white, cast on 12 sts and work 7 R in st st. K next R. Beginning with a K R, continue in st st to 12 cm or 4¾". Cast off.

Finishing: Work as for Jim for seams, stuffing, and features. Embroider anchor on pocket. Using blue, work backstitches between garter st ridges at neck. Sew on buttons as shown. For hair, cut 5 cm or 2" lengths of red yarn and knot into last 3 cm or 1¼" of head. Embroider freckles in red.

JACK

Additional Materials: Yarn: Remnants of white, blue, and red. St holder. Red pompon.

Legs: (make 2) Using red, cast on 24 sts and work in st st to 3 cm or 1¼". Cast off 4 sts at beginning of next 2 R — 16 sts. Work straight to 6 cm or 2½". Change to blue, casting on 4 sts at beginning of next 2 R — 24 sts. Work to 9 cm or 3½". Cast off.

Body: Using red, cast on 48 sts. K 1 R, then *K 2 R each in white, blue, white, and red, repeat from * to 4 cm or 1½". Place on st holder. For pocket, cast on 18 sts in red and work as for Body. Place these sts in front of center 18 Body sts and work across, knitting together 1 st from each set in center. Continue in garter st stripes, but work the front inset as for Johnny, using a separate ball of white and working in st st.

Head: At 8 cm or 3", work across all sts in st st, working 4 R blue, 2 R white, then in blue to 16 cm or 6¼". Cast off.

Arms: Using white, work as for Johnny, but work 4 R st st, 10 R garter st, then st st to end.

Finishing: Work as for Jim. Stuff legs and sew in position. Embroider anchor onto inset. Sew pompon to top of head.

The young explorer

These two colorful knitted playsuits will give baby plenty of room for movement.

FOR BOTH
Size: 9–12 months.
Basic Stitch: St st.
Tension: 28 sts and 40 R = 10 cm or 4".
Abbreviations: K = knit. P = purl. St(s) = stitch(es). R = row(s). Rnd(s) = round(s). St st = stocking or stockinette stitch.

BLUE SUIT
Materials Required:

200 gm or 8 oz blue, 50 gm or 2 oz white. Knitting needles and circular needle size 1 (Am) or 12 (Eng). 10 small buttons.
Stripe Sequence: 20 R blue, (2 R white, 18 R blue) 2 times, (3 R white, 17 R blue) 2 times, (4 R white and 16 R blue) 2 times, 1 R white, 6 R blue, 2 R white, 5 R blue, 3 R white, 4 R blue, 4 R white, 3 R blue, 5 R white, 2 R blue, 6 R white, 1 R blue, and remainder in white.

DIRECTIONS
Suit: Back: Begin at right leg and using blue, cast on 34 sts and work 2 cm or 3/4" in K 1, P 1 rib. Continue in Basic Pattern in Stripe Sequence to 17 cm or 6 3/4". Increase 1 st at end of K R on every 4th R 3 times, 1 st at end of every 2nd R 3 times — 40 sts. Work to 22 cm or 8 1/2". Leave on st holder.
Work other leg to match, reversing shaping, then work straight on all 80 sts to 43 cm or 17".
Shape Armholes: At beginning of every R, cast off 3 sts 2 times, 2 sts 6 times, 1 st 4 times — 58 sts. Work 2 cm or 3/4" straight, then increase 1 st each end of next R and every 4th R 5 times — 70 sts. *At the same time*, at 52 cm or 20 1/2" shape neck by casting off center 24 sts and working on each side separately. At neck edge, in every 2nd R cast off 2 sts 2 times, and 1 st 1 time. *At the same time,* at 53 cm or 21" in every 2nd R at armhole edge, cast off 9 sts 2 times.
Front: Work to match Back, but shape neck at 49 cm or 19 1/4" by casting off center 14 sts and working on each side separately. At neck edge, in every 2nd R cast off 3 sts 1 time, 2 sts 2 times, and 1 st 3 times.
Finishing: Press work lightly. Join side and leg seams. Using circular needle, begin at lower edge of left armhole and pick up 35 sts to shoulder, 16 sts along shoulder, 52 sts from front neck edge, 16 sts along shoulder, 70 sts around right armhole, 16 sts along back shoulder, 42 sts from back neck, 16 sts from left back shoulder, 35 sts down other armhole edge. Work 3 rnds in K1, P1 rib over all sts, but in Rnd 1, work buttonholes in front shoulder sts thus: (rib 3, cast off 2 sts) 3 times, rib to other shoulder, and repeat buttonholes. In next rnd, cast on 2 sts in place of those cast off. Rib next rnd and cast off in rib. Sew on buttons.
Pullover: Back: Using blue, cast on 74 sts and work 2 cm or 3/4" in K 1, P 1 rib. Change to st st and work to 10 cm or 4".
Shape Armholes: At beginning of every R, cast off 3 sts 2 times, 2 sts 2 times, and 1 st 8 times — 56 sts. Work straight to 20 cm or 8".
Shape Shoulders: At beginning of next 2 R, cast off 14 sts 2 times. Work 2 cm or 3/4" in rib on remaining 28 sts. Cast off in rib.
Front: Work as for Back to 17 cm or 6 3/4".
Shape Neck: Cast off center 8 sts and work on each side separately. At neck edge, in every 2nd R cast off 3 sts 1 time, 2 sts 3 times, and 1 st 1 time. When work measures 20 cm or 8", cast off 14 sts at beginning of next armhole edge R.
Sleeves: Using blue, cast on 28 sts and work 2 cm or 3/4" in K 1, P 1 rib. Change to st st, increasing 1 st each end of every 5th R 11 times — 50 sts. Work straight to 17 cm or 6 3/4".
Shape Top: At beginning of every R, cast off 3 sts 2 times, 2 sts 6 times, 1 st 4 times, 2 sts 6 times, 3 sts 2 times. Cast off remaining 10 sts.
Finishing: Press lightly on wrong side. With right side facing, pick up and K 35 sts along neck edge and work 2 cm or 3/4" in K 1, P 1 rib. Cast off in rib. Pick up and K 15 sts along back shoulder edges and work in rib for 4 R. Cast off in rib. Work front shoulders in rib in the same way, but in R 2: rib 3, cast off 2, rib 5, cast off 2, rib to end. In next R, cast on 2 sts in place of those cast off. Sew on buttons.

RED SUIT
Materials Required: Yarn: (see sample for Blue Suit) 150 gm or 6 oz red, 100 gm or 4 oz white. Knitting needles, circular needle, double-pointed needles size 1 (Am) or 12 (Eng). 6 buttons. Crochet hook size B (Am) or 2.00 (Eng).
Stripe Sequence: *4 R white in st st, then 2 R red in garter st.

DIRECTIONS
Suit: Back: Begin at right leg and using white, cast on 32 sts and work in Stripe Sequence, with cast-on R as first white R and repeating from * 2 times. Then work 4 R in white, thus ending after a right side R. Change to st st and continue in red, beginning with a P R, and at beginning of R increase 1 st in every 6th R 3 times. *At the same time,* at end of R increase 1 st in every 4th R 3 times and on every 2nd R 3 times — 41 sts.
Work straight to 8 cm or 3" and leave on st holder. Work other leg to match, then work across all sts to 29 cm or 11 1/2".
Shape Armholes: At beginning of every R, cast off 3 sts 2 times, 2 sts 6 times, 1

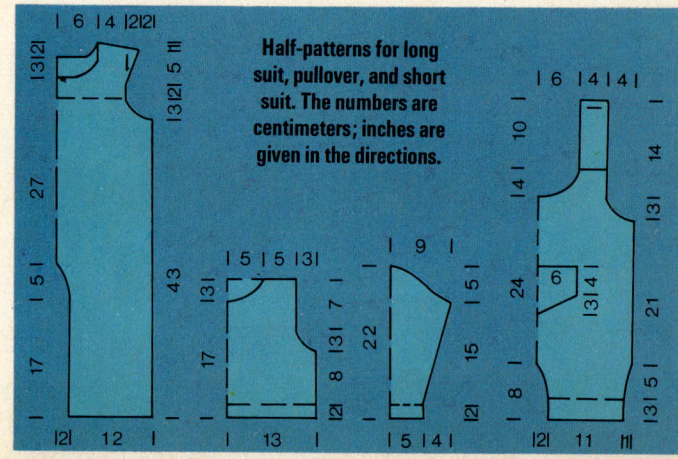

Half-patterns for long suit, pullover, and short suit. The numbers are centimeters; inches are given in the directions.

672

st 4 times — 60 sts. Continue straight to 32 cm or 12½".

Shape Neck: Cast off center 14 sts, and work on each side separately. At neck edge, in every 2nd R cast off 3 sts 1 time, 2 sts 2 times, and 1 st 4 times. Work straight on remaining 12 sts to 45 cm or 17¾". Work a buttonhole in next R: K 4, cast off 4 sts, K 4. In next R, cast on 4 sts in place of those cast off. Work straight for 1 cm or ⅜". Cast off.

Front: Work as for Back to 36 cm or 14". Cast off remaining 12 sts.

Pocket: Using white, cast on 4 sts and work in Stripe Sequence. Work 1 R straight, *cast on 2 sts at beginning of next 2 R and 3 sts at beginning of next 2 R, repeat from * 2 times more — 34 sts. Continue straight for 4 cm or 1½". Cast off.

Finishing: Press work lightly on wrong side. Join seams. Using crochet hook and red, work 1 rnd of double crochet around leg edges, shoulder, and neck edges. Sew on pocket as shown in picture. Sew on buttons.

Pullover: Working bottom border, cuffs, and neck edges in white and main part in Stripe Sequence, work to match Blue Pullover.

Socks: Using white, cast 10 sts onto each of 4 double-pointed needles and with 5th needle, work 2 cm or ¾" in K 1, P 1 rib. Continue in Stripe Sequence to 6 cm or 2½".

Shape Heel: Using red only, work in st st across 1st and 4th needles. Work 1 st less at end of next 10 rows, turning each R with yarn over needle. Now work 10 rows, working 1 st more at end of R each time, knitting together the extra st with the yarn-over-needle through back of loops. Work in rnds once more in Stripe Sequence for 6 cm or 2½".

Change to red only and work 8 rnds, decreasing 1 st at beginning of each needle by slip 1, K 1, pass slip st over. Cut yarn and draw through remaining 8 sts. Fasten off.

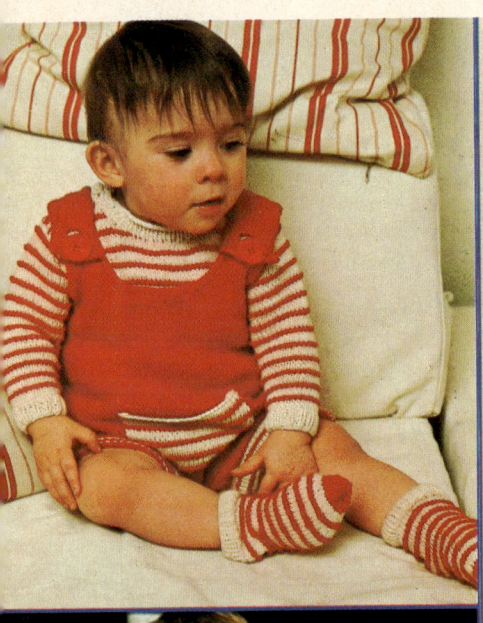

Left:
The red version has knee-length pants and a handy pocket for the young explorer. The pullover and socks are gaily striped for a color contrast.

The blue version has a plain pullover and ankle-length striped pants.

For the little people

Young inseparables will love these outfits, knitted in bright nursery colors and durable enough to see them through a day's play.

FOR BOTH

Sizes: Directions are for a 2-year-old. Changes for a 4-year-old are in brackets.
Basic Pattern: St st, using thicker needles.
Border Pattern: K 1, P 1 rib, using finer needles.
Stripe Sequence: 4 R each of blue, red or orange, green, and white.
Tension: 25 sts and 36 R = 10 cm or 4".
Abbreviations: K = knit. P = purl. St(s) = stitch(es). St st = stocking or stockinette stitch. R = row(s).

BIB SKIRT

Materials Required:

150 (200) gm or 6 (8) oz blue, 50 gm or 2 oz each red, green, and white [50 gm = 156 m or 170 yds]. Knitting needles sizes 2 and 0 (Am) or 11 and 14 (Eng). 2 buttons. 3 stitch holders.

DIRECTIONS

Back: Using blue and thicker needles, cast on 76 (86) sts and work 3 cm or 1¼" in st st for hem. Now continue in st st and Stripe Sequence 2 times, then continue in blue to 6 cm or 2½", ending after a P R. Decrease in next R thus: K 3, K 2 together, then K to last 5 sts, K 2 together, K 3. Decrease in same way on every 4th (6th) R 12 times — 50 (60) sts. Work straight to 23 (29) cm or 9" (11½"), ending after a P R. Leave sts on st holder.
Front: Work as for Back to 23 (29) cm or 9" (11½"), then straight for 2 cm or ¾".
Shape Armholes: Work in Stripe Sequence, but begin with red, and at beginning of every R cast off 3 (5) sts 2 times, 2 sts 4 (6) times, and 1 st each end of every 4th R 2 (3) times.
Work straight until the 2nd white (blue) stripe has been worked. Change to finer needles and blue, P next R on right side, then work 2 cm or ¾" in K 1, P 1 rib and cast off in rib.
Side Parts: (make 2) Using blue, cast on 54 (64) sts and work as for Back, leaving 28 (38) sts after decreases. Work to 23 (29) cm or 9" (11½") and leave on st holder.
Straps: Using blue, cast on 17 sts and work in K 1, P 1 rib to 1 cm or ⅜". Cast off center st and continue in rib separately on each set of 8 sts for 4 R. Work across all sts, casting on 1 st in center, and continue in rib for required length. Cast off in rib.
Finishing: Press lightly, then join seams. Using finer needles, pick up 31 (39) sts along each Front armhole edge, placing sts from st holders in between. Using blue, P first R on right side, then work in rib for 2 cm or ¾". Cast off in rib. Turn under hem at lower edges and sew down. Sew a button on either side of front rib, and sew on straps at Back, crossing them over to fasten at Front. If necessary, run a few rows of elastic thread through sides and back rib.

BIB PANTS

Materials Required: Yarn: (see sample for Bib Skirt) 150 (200) gm or 6 (8) oz blue, 50 gm or 2 oz each in orange, green, and white. Knitting needles sizes 2 and 0 (Am) or 11 and 14 (Eng). 2 buttons. Stitch holders.

DIRECTIONS

Back: Begin at right leg. Using blue and thicker needles, cast on 40 (46) sts and work in st st for 2 cm or ¾" for hem. Now work in st st and Stripe Sequence 2 times, then continue in blue. *At the same time,* at 4 cm or 1½" decrease 1 st at each end of next R and on every 18th (22nd) R 3 times — 32 (38) sts.
Now at right side edge (outside edge) increase 1 st in every 7th (9th) R 6 times and at left edge increase 1 st every 10th (12th) R 4 times — 42 (48) sts. Work to 32 (39) cm or 12½" (15¼"), then at left edge, shape for crotch by decreasing 1 st in every 2nd R 2 times and in every 4th R 2 times — 38 (44) sts. Work straight to 35 (42) cm or 13¾" (16½"), then leave work on st holder.
Work left leg as for right leg, reversing all shapings. Now work across both sets of 76 (88) sts and work straight for 2 cm or ¾", then decrease 1 st each end of next R and on every 12th (14th) R 4 times. Work straight to 51 (59) cm or 20" (23¼"). Leave remaining 66 (78) sts on st holder.
Front: Work as for Back to 51 (59) cm or 20" (23¼"), then beginning with an orange band work in Stripe Sequence, and at beginning of every R cast off 3 (5) sts 2 times, 2 sts 6 (8) times, 1 st 6 (10) times, and 1 st each end of every 4th R 3 times — 36 sts remain. For small size only, work straight for 2 more R — 2nd white (blue) stripe has been worked. Change to finer needles and with blue yarn, P first R, then work in rib for 2 cm or ¾". Cast off in rib.
Straps: Work as for Straps of Bib Skirt.
Finishing: Join seams. Work armhole borders as for Bib Skirt, but pick up 39 (47) sts along each armhole edge. Turn leg edges under and stitch down. Sew on Straps and buttons as for Bib Skirt.

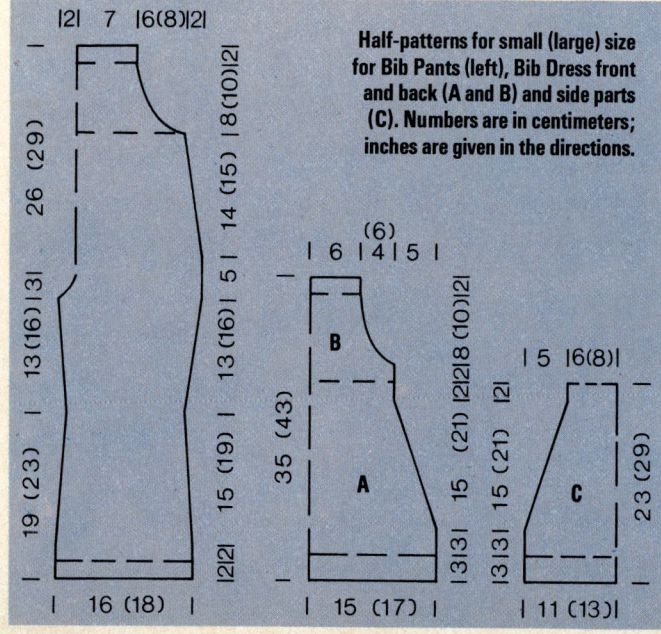

Half-patterns for small (large) size for Bib Pants (left), Bib Dress front and back (A and B) and side parts (C). Numbers are in centimeters; inches are given in the directions.

Both styles have buttoned shoulder straps for easy dressing and are roomy enough to suit the most active child.

Knitting

Soft stripes for play days

Here are four little pullovers in a soft, soft yarn. The pattern can be worked in any of the four different color and stripe variations.

Size: Directions are for 56 cm or 22" chest. Changes for 60 cm or 23½" chest are in brackets.

Materials Required:

Colors and quantities are given in individual directions. Knitting needles and a set of double-pointed needles size 2 (Am) or 11 (Eng). Stitch holder.

Basic Pattern: St st.
Tension: 22 sts and 36 R = 10 cm or 4".
Abbreviations: K = knit. P = purl. St(s) = stitch(es). R = row(s). Rnd(s) = round(s). St st = stocking or stockinette stitch.

PULLOVER 1

Materials Required: Yarn: 100 gm or 4 oz green, 50 gm or 2 oz white.
Color Sequence: Back: Work rib in white, then continue in green. Front: Work rib in white, then work in alternating stripe pattern of 4 R green and 4 R white. Sleeve: Work rib in white, then continue in green. Neckband: Work in white.

1 Knit the front in even stripes of white and green, the back and sleeves in plain green, and the ribbed cuffs and borders in white.

PULLOVER 2
Materials Required: Same as for Pullover 1.
Color Sequence: Back and Front: Work rib in white, then continue in green. When shaping for armhole, work 4 R each in white, green, then white. Continue in green. Sleeve: Work rib in white, then continue in green. Neckband: Work in white.

PULLOVER 3
Materials Required: Yarn: 50 gm or 2 oz each of blue, pink, and white.
Color Sequence: Back and Front: Work rib in pink, then work stripe sequence once thus: 4 R each white, pink, blue, white, pink, blue, white, pink. Continue in blue. Sleeve: Work rib in pink, then alternate stripes of 4 R each white, pink, and blue. Neckband: Work in white.

PULLOVER 4
Materials Required: Same as for Pullover 3.
Color Sequence: Back, Front, and Sleeves: Work rib in blue, then continue in alternating stripes of 4 R each of white, pink, white, and blue to end. Neckband: Work in blue.

*

DIRECTIONS
Note: Work in Color Sequence given in individual directions.
Back: Cast on 62 (66) sts and work 5 cm or 2" in K 1, P 1 rib. Continue straight in st st to 16 (18) cm or 6¼" (7").
Shape Armholes: At beginning of every R, cast off 2 sts 4 times and 1 st 10 times — 44 (48) sts. Work straight to 27 (30) cm or 10½" (11¾").
Shape Neck: Cast off center 14 sts and work on each side separately. At neck edge, in every 2nd R cast off 2 sts 1 time and 1 st 2 times. *At the same time,* at 28 (31) cm or 11" (12¼"), shape shoulder at armhole edge in every 2nd R by casting off 5 (6) sts 1 time and 6 (7) sts 1 time.
Front: Work armhole and shoulder shaping as for Back, but shape neck at 22 (25) cm or 8¾" (9¾"). Cast off center 6 sts and work on each side separately. At neck edge, in every 2nd R cast off 2 sts 2 times and 1 st 4 times.
Sleeves: Cast on 30 sts and work 4 cm or 1½" in K 1, P 1 rib. Change to st st and increase 1 st each end of every 9th R 7 (9) times — 44 (48) sts. Work straight to 22 (28) cm or 8¾" (11").
Shape Top: At beginning of every R cast off 3 (4) sts 2 times, 2 sts 4 times, 1 st 12 times, 2 sts 4 times, 3 (4) sts 2 times. Cast off remaining 4 sts.
Finishing: Join seams. Using double-pointed needles pick up and K 74 (80) sts around neck edge and work in rnds of K 1, P 1 rib for 4 cm or 1½". Cast off in rib. Fold neckband in half to wrong side and stitch neatly in place.

2 This version is in green with white borders. Add two white stripes across the front and back.

3 Work stripes on the front and back as far as the armholes, then continue in blue. Work the sleeves in alternating stripes.

4 The final variation is to work the pattern in stripes and the ribbed borders and cuffs in a plain color.

Half-patterns in small (large) sizes. The numbers are in centimeters; inch equivalents are in the directions.

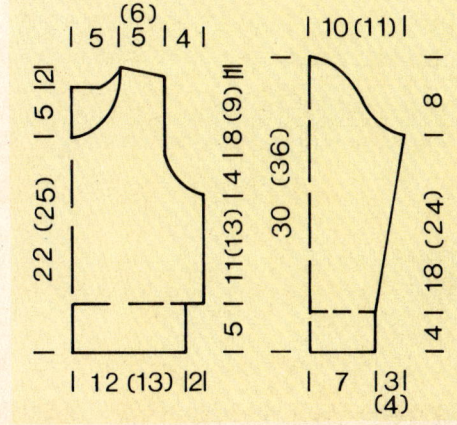

677

Team spirit

What a winner! Three pullovers in three sizes, with color and stripe variations, using speckled yarn.

Size: Directions are for 58 cm or 23" chest. Changes for 62 (66) cm or 24" (26") chest are in brackets.

Materials Required:

Quantities and colors are given in individual directions [50 gm = 86 m or 94 yds]. Knitting needles sizes 4 and 5 (Am) or 8 and 9 (Eng). Circular needle size 4 (Am) or 9 (Eng). St holder.

STYLE 1
Yarn: 100 gm or 4 oz each in bright red, dark red, and beige.
Color Sequence: *6 R bright red; 2 R each beige, dark red, and beige; 6 R dark red; 2 R each beige, bright red, beige; repeat from *.

STYLE 2
Yarn: 100 gm or 4 oz each light blue, dark blue, beige.
Color Sequence: *6 R light blue, 2 R beige, 6 R dark blue, 2 R beige, repeat from *.

STYLE 3
Yarn: 100 gm or 4 oz each light green and dark green, 100 (100: 150) gm or 4 (4:6) oz beige mixture.
Color Sequence: *6 R light green; 2 R each beige, dark green, beige, dark green, light green; 6 R dark green; 2 R each beige, light green, beige, light green, dark green; repeat from *.

Basic Stitch: St st.
Tension: 18 sts and 28 R = 10 cm or 4".
Abbreviations: K = knit. P = purl. St(s) = stitch(es). St st = stocking or stockinette st. R = row(s). Rnd(s) = round(s).

DIRECTIONS
Back: Using finer needles cast on 54 (58:62) sts and work in K 1, P 1 rib for 4 (5:6) cm or 1½" (2":2½"). Change to thicker needles and work in st st and Color Sequence as given for each style to 35 (38:41) cm or 13¾" (15":16").
Shape Neck: Cast off center 16 (16:18) sts and work on each side separately. At neck edge, in every 2nd R cast off 2 sts 1 time and 1 st 1 time. Cast off remaining 16 (18:19) sts.
Front: Work as Back to 30 (33:35) cm or 11¾" (13":13¾").
Shape Neck: Cast off center 8 (8:10) sts and work on each side separately. At neck edge, in every 2nd R cast off 2 sts 1 time and 1 st 5 times. Continue straight until work measures same as Back to shoulder. Cast off remaining 16 (18:19) sts.
Sleeves: Using finer needles, cast on 28 (32:36) sts and work 4 (5:6) cm or 1½" (2":2½") in K 1, P 1 rib. Change to thicker needles and work in st st and Color Sequence, increasing 1 st each end of every 10th (11th:12th) R 8 times — 44 (48:52) sts. Work straight to 34 (38:42) cm or 13½" (15":16½"). Cast off.
Neckband: Using circular needle and beige, cast on 88 (88:96) sts and work 2 cm or ¾" in K 1, P 1 rib.
Finishing: Press work on wrong side with a warm iron over damp cloth. Join all seams, then sew on Neckband.

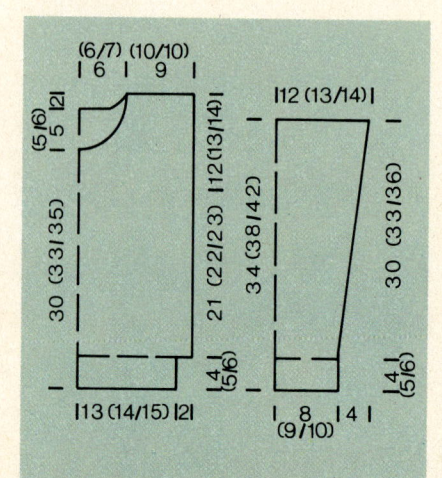

Half-pattern for small (medium: large) size. Numbers are centimeters; inches are in the directions.

Style 1

Style 2

Style 3

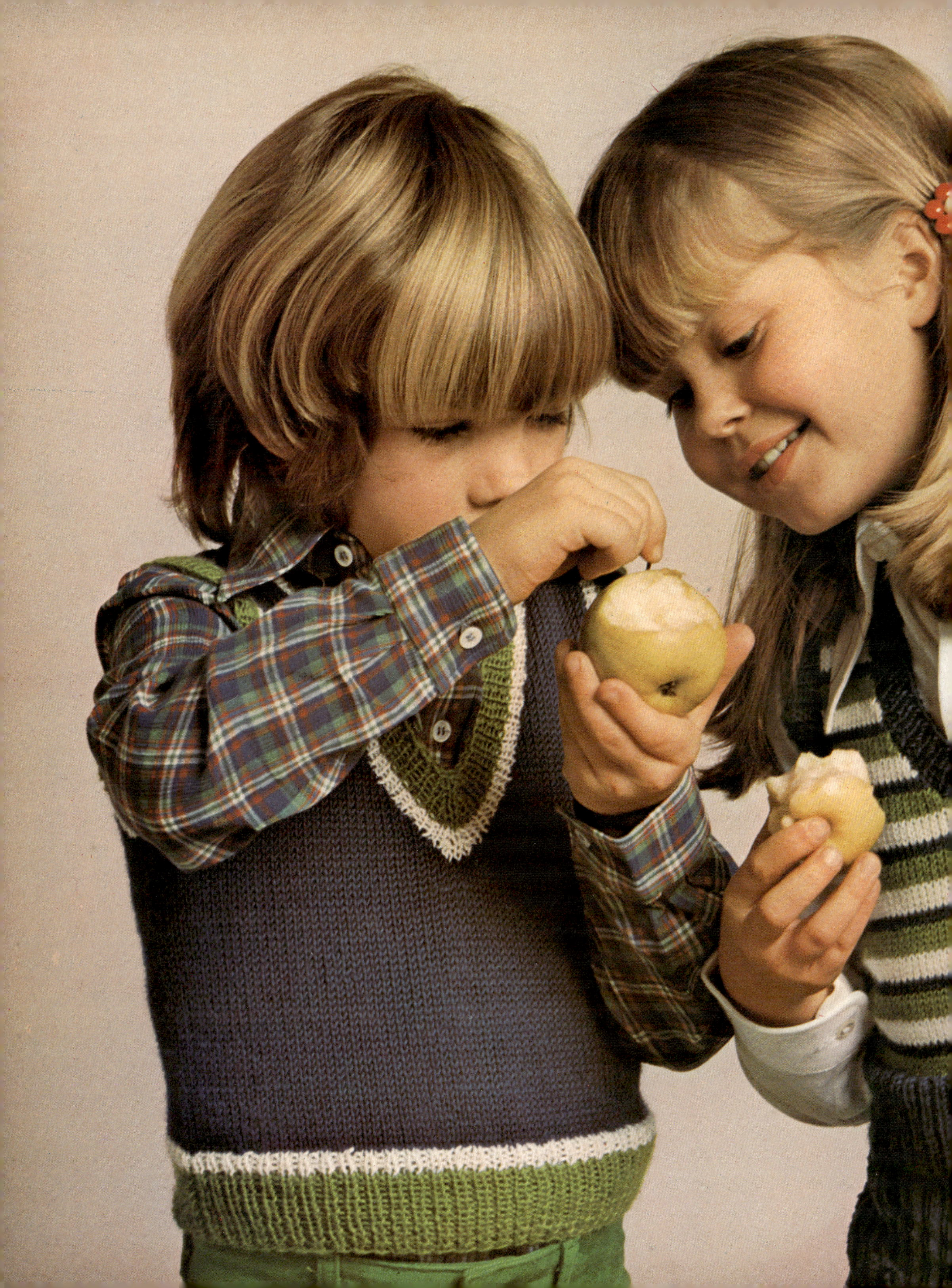

Knitting

Made from the same pattern

Romper tops

Comfortable play tops will keep little ones warm when there's a chill in the air.

FOR BOTH
Size: Directions are for 58 cm or 23" chest. Changes for 62 cm or 24" chest are in brackets.

Materials Required:

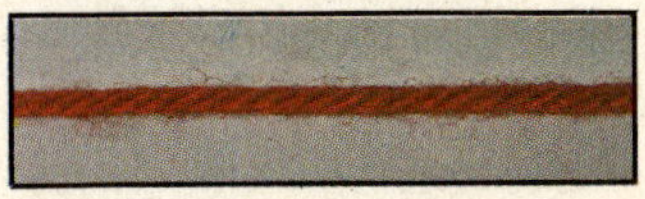

Blue Top: 50 (100) gm or 2 (4) oz blue, 50 gm or 2 oz green, and a small ball of white.

Striped Top: 50 gm or 2 oz each blue, green, and white.

Knitting needles and a set of double-pointed needles size 2 (Am) or 11 (Eng).

Basic Stitch: Stocking or stockinette stitch.

Border Rib: K 1, P 1.

Color Sequence (for Striped Top): 4 R green, 2 R blue, 4 R white.

Tension: 25 sts and 36 R = 10 cm or 4".

Abbreviations: St(s) = stitch(es). R = row(s). Rnd(s) = round(s). K = knit. P = purl. St st = stocking or stockinette stitch.

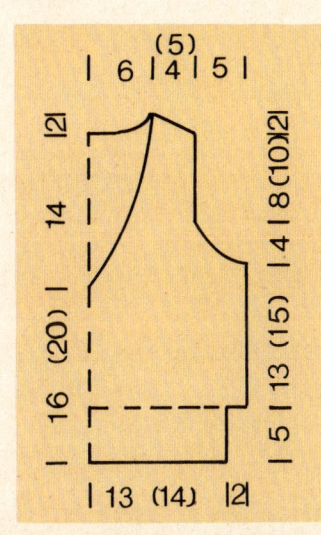

The measurements are in centimeters; inch equivalents are in the directions.

BLUE TOP
Back: Using green, cast on 74 (80) sts and work 4 cm or $1\frac{1}{2}$" in Border Rib. Work 4 R in white. Change to blue and work in st st to 18 (20) cm or 7" (8").

Shape Armholes: Cast off 3 sts at beginning of next 2 R, 2 sts at beginning of next 6 R, and decrease 1 st at beginning of next 6 R — 50 (56) sts. Work straight to 30 (34) cm or $11\frac{3}{4}$" ($13\frac{1}{2}$").

Shape Shoulder and Neck: Cast off center 24 sts, then work each side separately. At neck edge, cast off 2 sts once and 1 st once. *At the same time,* at armhole edge, cast off 3 (4) sts 2 times and 4 (5) sts 1 time.

Front: Work to match Back to 16 (20) cm or $6\frac{1}{4}$" (8").

Divide for Neck: Decrease 1 st at neck edge on every 3rd R 8 times, then on every 4th R 7 times. *At the same time,* shape armhole and shoulder to match Back.

Finishing: Press work on wrong side. Join seams. Using set of double-pointed needles and white pick up 118 (128) sts around neck and work in Border Rib; work 3 rnds white and 2 cm or $\frac{3}{4}$" green. *At the same time,* at V, decrease 1 st either side of the center st in every 2nd rnd. Cast off in rib. Using white, pick up 74 (86) sts around each armhole and work in rnds to match neckband — 3 rnds white and 2 cm or $\frac{3}{4}$" green.

STRIPED TOP
Follow instructions as for Blue Top, but work the borders in blue and main part in Color Sequence.

A cardigan in afghan crochet

Crochet

A special project

Size: Directions are for 88 cm or 34½" bust. Changes for 96 cm or 37½" bust are in brackets.

Materials Required:

300 (350) gm or 11 (13) oz navy, 100 gm or 4 oz each red and turquoise [50 gm = 200 m or 220 yds]. Crochet hook size D. Afghan crochet hook size F. 5 buttons.

Basic Pattern: Afghan crochet. **R 1:** (right side) Draw up 1 loop through each st of the previous R. Do not turn work. Yarn over and draw through 1st st, then * yarn over hook, draw through 2 loops on hook, and repeat from * to end. In all following R, draw up loops through the vertical thread of previous R.

Color Sequence: *3 R each of turquoise, red and navy. Repeat from *.

Border Pattern: Sc. Work into 2nd st from hook, then 1 sc into each st to end, turn with 1 ch.

Tension: 24 sts and 20 double R = 10 cm or 4".

Abbreviations: Ch = chain. Sc = single crochet. St(s) = stitch(es). R = row(s).

DIRECTIONS

Back: Using navy, make 115 (125) ch and work 4 cm or 1½" in Border Pattern. Change to Basic Pattern, following Color Sequence and decrease 1 st on each side in every 6th R 5 times — 104 (114) sts. Now increase 1 st in every 10th R 3 times — 110 (120) sts. Continue straight to 39 (40) cm or 15⅜" (15¾").

Shape Armholes: In next R, slip-st along 3 (4) sts, crochet to last 3 (4) sts and leave these unworked, then decrease 3 (4) sts at each end of R when looping off. Decrease 2 sts each end of next R, then decrease 1 (2) st(s) each end of next 2 R and 1 st each end of following 4 R — 82 (88) sts. Continue straight to 57 (59) cm or 22½" (23¼").

Shape Neck: Leave center 26 sts unworked and work on each side separately. Now at neck edge on every R, decrease 2 sts 3 times and 1 st 2 times. *At the same time* at 58 (60) cm or 22¾" (23½"), in every R at armhole edge, decrease 5 sts 3 (1) time(s) and 5 (6) sts 1 (3) time(s).

Left Front: Using navy, make 54 (59) ch and work 4 cm or 1½" in sc. Change to Basic Pattern and work in Color Sequence, shaping side, armhole, and shoulder as for Back. *At the same time,* at 37 cm or 14½", in every R at front edge decrease 1 st 6 times, 1 st in every 2nd R 6 times, and 1 st in every 3rd R 5 times.

Right Front: Work as for Left Front, reversing all shapings.

Sleeves: Using navy, make 59 (63) ch and work 4 cm or 1½" in sc. Continue in navy in Basic Pattern, increasing 1 st each end of every 5th R 15 times — 88 (92) sts. Work straight to 45 cm or 17¾".

Shape Top: At each end of every R, decrease 5 sts 1 time, 2 sts 3 times, 1 st 5 (6) times, 1 st each end of every 2nd R 4 times. In every R, decrease 1 st 5 (6) times, 2 sts 3 times, 5 sts 1 time — 16 sts remain. Fasten off.

Finishing: Join all seams. Using navy, work 61 sc along each straight part of front, 46 (52) sc to shoulder and 37 sc along back neck edge. Work in sc, working 2 sc into corner sts at beginning of front shaping in every 2nd R, until 2 cm or ¾". Work 5 buttonholes in Right Front band in next R, working over 3 sts, placing the first one 2 cm or ¾" from lower edge, and 4 more at 6.5 cm or 2½" intervals. Still increasing at corners, continue in sc until band measures 4 cm or 1½". Fasten off. Sew on the buttons.

If you have not yet added afghan crochet to your repertoire of techniques, now is the time. A special hook is used and the result is a firm fabric that is rather like knitting in appearance. Try your new skills for this subtly striped cardigan with a V-neck and plain sleeves.

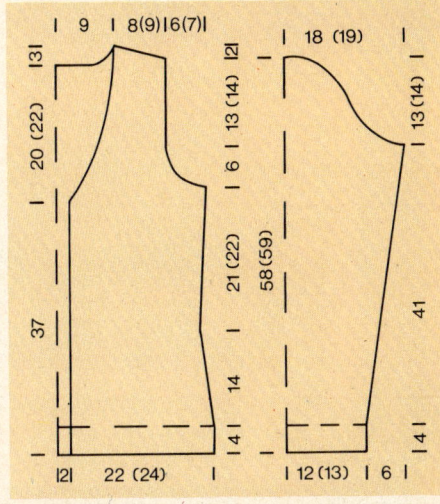

Half-pattern for small (large) size. The numbers are centimeters; inches are in the directions.

How-to

Afghan crochet

1 To begin the afghan crochet after a border, change to afghan crochet hook and draw up a loop from each single crochet of previous row.

2 Do not turn the work. Yarn over the hook and draw it through the first loop on the hook . . .

3 . . . *yarn over the hook and draw through the next two loops on the hook, repeat from * across.

4 In all further rows, insert the hook under the vertical thread of the stitch in the previous row and draw the yarn through. When you have picked up loops across, work them as shown in 2 and 3.

5 For decreases at the right edge, slip-stitch across the required number of stitches. At the left edge, leave the required number unworked.

6 To decrease when working off the loops, draw yarn through 2 loops at left edge and draw yarn through 3 loops for other decreases at left end. At the right edge, draw yarn through 3 loops.

How-to

Crochet stitches that look like knitting

Crocheted knit stitch

1 Crocheted knitting stitch can only be worked from the right side in rows or rounds. Single crochet stitches are worked by inserting the hook under the whole stitch.

2 To increase inside the row or round, first work single crochet as shown in photograph 1, then work another single crochet under the upper two threads of same stitch in previous row.

3 The brims of the hats can be finished with a round of slip stitches worked from the right side so that the stitches lie next to the stitches of the last round of single crochet.

Afghan knit stitch

1 From the right side, insert the hook between the front and back of the stitch.

2 Pass the yarn over the hook and draw the loop through the stitches. Leave the loop on the hook.

3 Return row: yarn over, draw through 1 loop, * yarn over, draw through 2 loops, repeat from *.

4 When changing colors, draw the new color through the last two loops, crossing strands.

Crochet

Using two different techniques

Set for winter

Size: Hat: 54 cm or 21¼" around head.
Scarf: 24 cm x 200 cm or 9½" x 79".

Materials Required:

[50 gm = 75 m or 80 yds].
Hat: 100 gm or 4 oz dark blue, 50 gm or 2 oz each of white and blue *or* 50 gm or 2 oz each of rust, white, and petrol blue. Narrow elastic. Scarf: 200 gm or 8 oz dark blue, 100 gm or 4 oz each of white and blue *or* 150 gm or 6 oz each of rust, white, and petrol blue. Both: Crochet hook and afghan crochet hook size K.

Basic Pattern: Hat: Sc in rnds with every sc worked under complete st (see How-to). Every rnd begins with 1 ch and ends with a slip stitch into ch.
Scarf: R 1: (right side) Draw 1 loop from each ch of foundation R, leaving st on hook. R 2: (right side – do not turn after previous R). Yarn over hook and draw through a loop, then yarn over hook and draw through 2 loops, continue drawing yarn through 2 loops at a time to end. R 3: (right side) Insert hook and draw loop from in between front and back of st to end (see How-to). R 4: (right side) Repeat R 2. Repeat R 3 and 4.

Color Sequence: Hat: *1 rnd each dark blue, white, blue *or* rust, white, petrol blue. Repeat from *.
Scarf: *1 R from right to left and return R from left to right in same color in dark blue, white, blue *or* rust, white, petrol blue. Repeat from *.

Tension: 11 sts and 14 rnds or R = 10 cm or 4". Note that 2 R of scarf, count as 1 when measuring for tension.

Abbreviations: Ch = chain. Sc = single crochet. St(s) = stitch(es). R = row(s). Rnd(s) = round(s).

DIRECTIONS

Hat: Make 3 ch in dark blue or rust and join into a ring with a slip stitch. Follow Basic Pattern and Color Sequence, increasing thus: Rnd 1: Work 6 sc into ring. Rnd 2: Work 2 sc into each st (see How-to) – 12 sts. Rnd 3: Sc, working 2 sc into every 2nd st – 18 sts. Rnd 4: Sc, working 2 sc into every 3rd st – 24 sts. Rnd 5: Increase in every 3rd st – 32 sts. Rnd 6: Sc. Rnd 7: Increase in every 4th st – 40 sts. Rnd 8: Sc. Rnd 9: Increase in every 5th st – 48 sts. Rnd 10: Sc. Rnd 11: Increase in every 6th st – 56 sts. Continue straight for 16 rnds. Rnd 28: Increase in every 4th st – 70 sts. Rnd 29: Increase in every 7th st – 80 sts. Work straight to Rnd 36, then work 1 rnd of slip stitch (see How-to). Fasten off. Thread elastic through Rnd 27.

Scarf: Using dark blue or rust, and using afghan hook, work in Basic Pattern and Color Sequence, working 2 R of each color for 200 cm or 79", ending with 2 R dark blue or rust. Cut yarn into 20 cm or 8" lengths and work a knotted fringe along each edge, working in dark blue for blue scarf and in the 3 colors for other scarf.

The scarves are worked in afghan crochet stitch for an unusual effect.

These long scarves have matching pull-on hats and are ideal for cold, wintry weather. The scarves are worked in afghan crochet and the hats in single crochet.

687

In afghan crochet
Blanket coverage

Curl up and relax in style with the aid of this handsome coverlet crocheted in pure wool and embroidered with cross-stitch designs.

Size: About 130 cm x 210 cm or 51" x 83".

Materials Required:

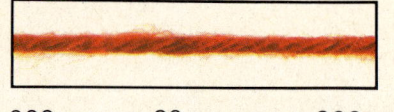

900 gm or 32 oz green, 800 gm or 29 oz white, 700 gm or 25 oz rust, 650 gm or 23 oz brown [50 gm = 102 m or 112 yds]. Afghan crochet hook size J. Large eyed, blunt tipped needle.

Basic Pattern: Afghan crochet. On right side, draw a loop through each upright st of the previous R. Do not turn work. Yarn over and draw through 1 st, then *yarn over and through next 2 sts, repeat from * to end. This is counted as 1 row.

Embroidery Pattern: Each color sign = 1 cross stitch over an afghan stitch. Grey represents white.

Tension: 16 sts and 15 R = 10 cm or 4".

Abbreviations: St(s) = stitch(es). Ch = chain. Tr = treble. R = row(s). Sc = single crochet.

DIRECTIONS

The coverlet is worked in separate strips which are sewn together afterward.

Rust Strip (make 6): Work 13 ch and, working into 3rd ch from hook for 1st st, work 199 R in Basic

Pattern. Fasten off.

Green Strip (make 2): Work 51 ch and work 199 R in Basic Pattern. Fasten off.

Brown, White, Brown Strip (make 3): Using brown make 14 ch, using white make 21 ch, then with another ball of brown work 16 ch (last 2 ch for turning ch). Work in Basic Pattern and at color changeover, always work last st in the following color. Work to the second half of the 4th R, then work to 1 st before color changeover, make 1 tr 3 R lower (see How-to), then at beginning of the white strip make another tr back into the 1st R. Work other color changeover in the same way. Work tr every 3rd R, and work 199 R in all. Fasten off.

Finishing: Embroider the green strips following the large cross-stitch diagram (21 sts and R form one complete pattern). Work 1 cross-stitch over 1 afghan st, working from the 15th–35th sts across. Begin the 1st motif in the 9th R from lower edge, and 6 more motifs each 6 R apart.

Next embroider the rust strips, following the small motif (5 sts and R form one complete pattern). Work motif on 4th–8th sts across and begin in the 10th R from lower edge. Work motif alternately in green and white 17 times with 6 rows between each motif. Now work around all strips using rust and working in sc.

Place strips in color sequence thus: rust, brown-white-brown, rust, green, rust, brown-white-brown, rust, green, rust, brown-white-brown, rust. Overcast all strips together with double rust strand, picking up both threads of sc. Finally sc all around the outer edge to give a neat border.

The coverlet is easy to assemble, as it is crocheted in separate strips and then sewn together.

Right: Large motif for the dark-green strips.
Below: Small motif for the rust strips.

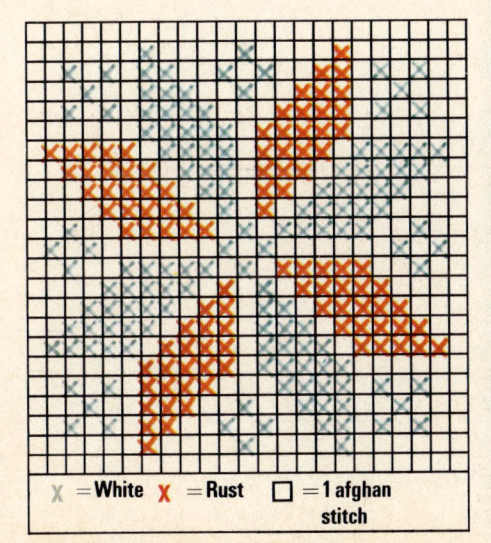

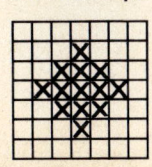

X = White   X = Rust   ☐ = 1 afghan stitch

How-to

Accentuated color change

Trebles are worked at the beginning and end of color areas in every 3rd row of the afghan crochet. Begin to work the trebles in the 4th row. Work to last loop of 1st color, yarn over twice and continue as shown below, but work under upright thread of stitch 3 rows below the previously worked stitch.

1 For trebles worked in the left-hand color, insert the hook under the upright thread of the stitch in front of the previously worked treble.

2 Work the treble. With the new color, work the last loop of the old color with the first loop of the new color.

3 For the trebles worked in the right-hand color, always work under the first upright thread of the stitch behind the previously worked treble.

Armchair traveler

Spread a little warmth by crocheting this splendidly-textured wrap for all those who love their armchair comfort! A base is first crocheted in beige and dark brown and then toning strands of beige and brown are woven through the spaces.

Size: About 95 cm x 135 cm or 37½" x 53" – including fringes.

Materials Required:

For Basic Pattern: 250 gm or 9 oz each of beige and dark brown.

For weaving: 200 gm or 8 oz each of beige and brown. Crochet hook size K.

Basic Pattern: R 1: (right side) Work 1 dc into 6th ch from hook, *skip 1 ch, 1 dc into next ch, repeat from * to end, turn with 3 ch. R 2: * 1 ch, 1 dc on next dc, repeat from * to end, working last dc into top of turning ch, turn with 3 ch. Repeat R 2.

Color Sequence: Alternately 3 R each of beige and dark brown.

Tension: 11 sts and 5 R = 10 cm or 4".

Abbreviations: Ch = chain. Dc = double crochet. R = row(s).

DIRECTIONS

Using dark brown, make 111 ch and work Basic Pattern in Color Sequence 8 times, then work another 3 R in brown – 51 R. Fasten off. For the weaving strands, cut 27 brown and 27 beige strands each about 300 cm or 118" long. Double the threads and draw through the filet crochet base with the hook. For easy working, make a loop in the doubled yarn and place round prong of hook, pull tightly. Then using the other end of the hook, weave through the spaces as shown below. Draw through the strands in an alternating color sequence of 3 double strands brown, 3 double strands beige. Leave equal long ends free at each edge for fringe. Cut the folded ends and knot together 2 strands, taking 1 strand from each of adjacent pairs (see the photograph below).

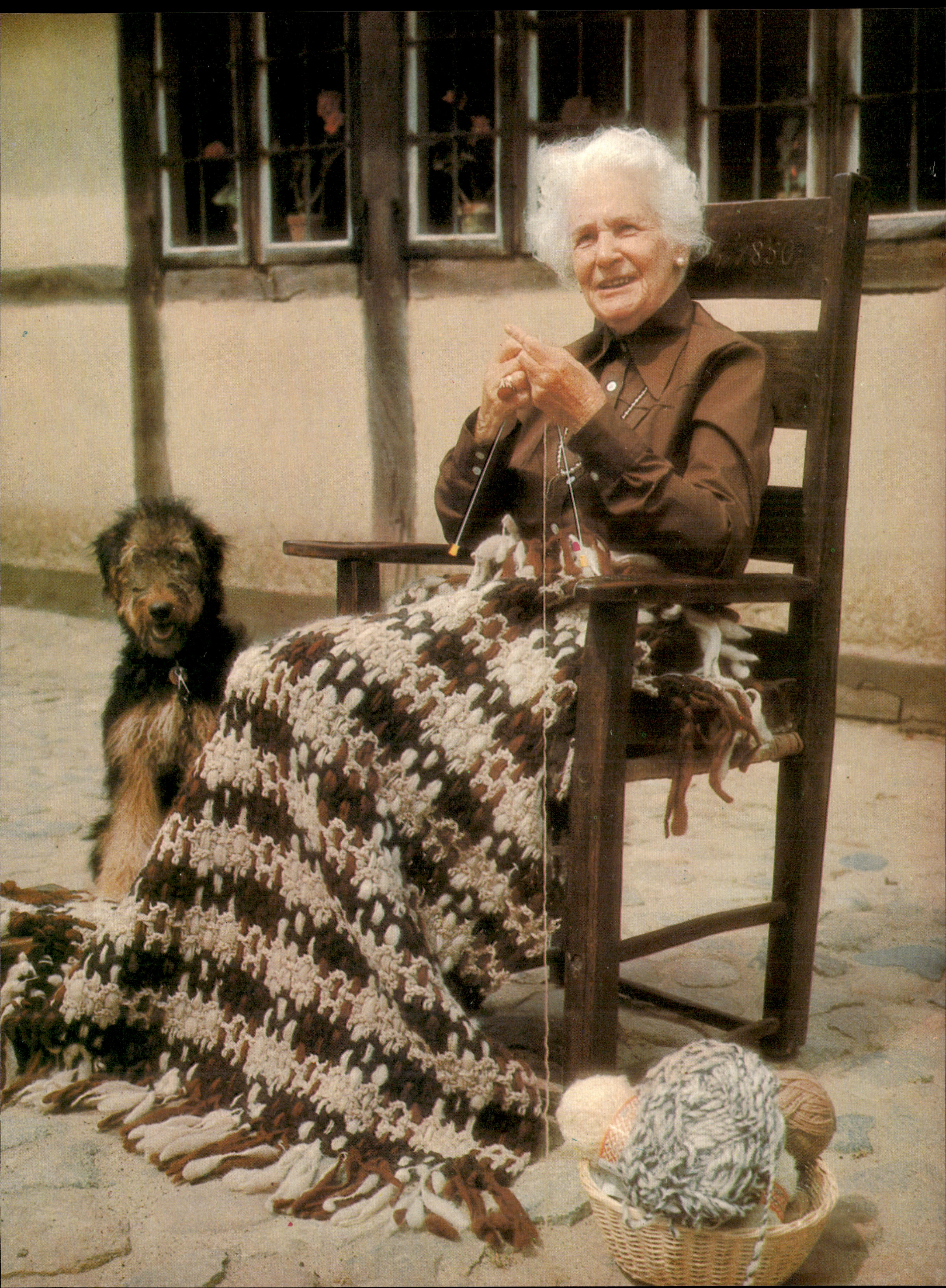

Square it with granny

For a dazzling centerpiece that will be equally appropriate both outdoors and indoors, crochet our exotic patchwork rug in hard-wearing sisal. Sisal is an ideal material for a floor covering, as it is tough enough to withstand wear and tear from feet walking over it all day. The rug is crocheted in separate squares, which are then sewn together. This means that the project may be completed in stages and will fit in with your other activities. You also have great freedom of choice in determining the final size and color scheme of the rug. You may be as exuberant with colors as you wish; the brighter, the better. A blending of bold colors make the rug versatile enough to fit in anywhere. Each square is worked in two colors, and a single-color border is crocheted around the completed rug. Beginners will have no difficulty with this project, which is worked with a very large crochet hook. If you have difficulty in obtaining the colors you want, dye the sisal with a hot- or cold-water dye. In this way you will be able to experiment with a great many color choices.

Size: About 125 cm or 50" square for a rug 5 squares wide and 5 squares long.

Materials Required:
Sisal: 4 balls blue, 3 balls each brown, light green, red, yellow, orange, 5 balls dark green. Crochet hooks size J for border and size 13 for squares.

Tension: Each square measures about 25 cm or 10" square.

Abbreviations: Ch = chain. Sc = single crochet. Dc = double crochet. St(s) = stitch(es). Rnd(s) = round(s).

DIRECTIONS

The Square: (25 required) Using 1st color, make 6 ch and join into a ring with a slip st.

Rnd 1: 3 ch (as 1st dc), 2 dc in ring, *3 ch, 3 dc, repeat from * into ring 2 times more, 3 ch, join with a slip st to 3rd ch at beginning. Join 2nd color in last st, tighten, and turn work.

Rnd 2: *Into 1st ch loop, work 3 dc, 3 ch, 3 dc, 1 ch, repeat from * 3 times more, join with a slip st. Now join 1st color with 1 ch in the last st, and turn work.

Rnd 3: *3 dc in ch loop, 1 ch, 3 dc, 3 ch, 3 dc in corner 3-ch loop, 1 ch, repeat from * 3 times, join with a slip st. Join 2nd color with 1 ch, turn.

Rnd 4: *3 dc in ch loop, 1 ch, 3 dc, 3 ch, 3 dc in corner loop, 1 ch, 3 dc in next ch loop, 1 ch, repeat from * all around, join with a slip st.

Rnd 5: Work sc in each dc and each 1-ch loop, working 4 sc into corner ch loops. Fasten off.

Finishing: Place squares, right sides together (the right side is the side where the sts of 1st color lie uppermost). With a needle and matching strand, sew the squares together at outer edge. Using blue, work in sc around outer edges, working 2 sc into corners. Break off blue, join dark green, and work a dc in each sc around rug, working 2 dc in sc at corners. Fasten off. Sew in all strand ends carefully to get a neat finish.

Here you see the seven colors we used to create a vivid multi-colored rug. For a more restrained look, choose two toning colors with one other color used for the outer border.

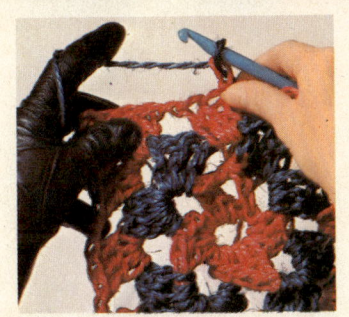

When crocheting, you should wear a leather glove on the hand that holds the sisal in order to protect your skin. Here the new color is inserted into the last stitch.

When you have finished each square, dampen it with cold water.

Now pull it into a perfect square shape to counteract the stretching caused by the crocheting, and place the square under a board that is weighted down with books.

The squares are placed together with the right sides facing and sewn together along the edges with a thick darning needle. Overcast, inserting needle into two outer threads only.

Crochet

Patchwork squares in paintbox colors

Start with one and you're on your way

Let your imagination run riot! Just crochet happily on, making piles and piles of squares in all sorts of color combinations and patterns, and then join them together for a fantastic bedspread! Somehow, bold, distinctive colors and designs never seem to clash when combined in this way.

Flowers bloom in abundance on this colorful cover. Three-dimensional roses are worked in Irish crochet in bright rose-like colors or in wild combinations for fantasy flowers.

How-to

Joining squares

With single crochet: Working from the right side, insert the hook under the lower threads of the edge stitches in each square and work single crochet in the usual way.

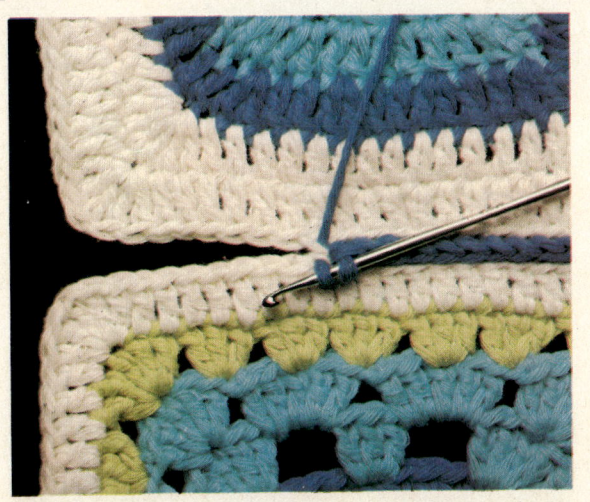

With chain stitch: Working from the wrong side, insert the hook under the upper threads of the edge stitches in each square and work chain stitch in the usual way.

With overcasting: Working from the wrong side, insert the needle under the upper threads of the edge stitches in each square and work overcasting stitches in the usual way.

IRISH ROSE SQUARES

Abbreviations: St(s) = stitches. Rnd(s) = rounds. Ch = chain. Sc = single crochet. Hdc = half double crochet. Dc = double crochet.

DIRECTIONS

Make 8 ch and join into a ring with a slip stitch. <u>Rnd 1:</u> 6 ch, *1 dc into ring, 3 ch, repeat from * 6 times more. Join with a slip st into 3rd of 6 ch (8 spaces). <u>Rnd 2:</u> (1 sc, 1 hdc, 4 dc, 1 hdc, 1 sc) into each 3-ch space (8 petals). Slip st along back of 1st petal to lower edge of 1st dc. <u>Rnd 3:</u> (work into the back of rnd 2) *5 ch, 1 sc into 1st dc of next petal, inserting the hook into the back of the stitch, repeat from * all around. <u>Rnd 4:</u> (1 sc, 1 hdc, 6 dc, 1 hdc, 1 sc) into each 5-ch space. <u>Rnd 5:</u> *7 ch, 1 sc into 1st dc of next petal, inserting the hook into the back of the stitch, repeat from * all around. <u>Rnd 6:</u> (1 sc, 1 hdc, 6 dc, 1 hdc, 1 sc) into each 7-ch space. <u>Rnd 7:</u> Join yarn to space between petals, (3 dc, 1 ch, 3 dc) into same space, *2 ch, 1 sc into center of next petal, 2 ch, 3 dc into space between petals, 2 ch, 1 sc into center of next petal, 2 ch, (3 dc, 1 ch, 3 dc) into space between petals, repeat from * 3 times, omitting last 3 dc, 1 ch, 3 dc. Join with a slip st in top of 1st dc and slip-stitch along to next 1-ch. <u>Rnd 8:</u> *(3 dc, 1 ch, 3 dc) into 1-ch space, (2 ch, 3 dc) into next 4 2-ch spaces, 2 ch, repeat from * all around. Join with slip stitch.

In all following rnds, work 3 dc, 2 ch into each 2-ch space along each side and 3 dc, 1 ch, 2 dc into each corner.

Patchwork can be made up of a wide variety of squares and still give a unified effect of color or design.

Size: 20 cm or 8" square.
Materials Required:

50 gm or 2 oz cotton yarn of one color for each pot holder. Crochet hook size F.
Basic Pattern: Sc, with 1 ch to turn.
Abbreviations: Ch = chain. Sc = single crochet. R = row(s).

DIRECTIONS
Make 12 ch and join into a ring with a slip stitch. Work 18 sc into a ring, join the round with a slip stitch, and work 1 ch to turn.
R 1 (right side): 1 sc into each of next 4 sc, 3 sc into next sc, 1 sc into each of next 4 sc, 1 ch, turn. R 2: 1 sc into each of next 5 sc, 3 sc into next sc (center sc), 1 sc into each of next 5 sc, 1 ch, turn. R 3: Inserting hook into the back loop of sc, work 6 sc, 3 sc in center sc, 6 sc, 1 ch, turn.
Repeat R 2 and 3, increasing the number of sc worked and working 3 sc into each center sc until side edges measure 20 cm or 8". Fasten off.

Pretty practical!

These colorful pot holders will be a cheerful addition to any kitchen and the texture of the crocheted cotton will protect your hands when handling hot dishes and pots. They're useful and decorative gifts for friends and they're popular items to make for local bazaars.

Popular styles in poplin

Illustrated Sewing 21

The pattern for this jacket and coat in sizes C and E, are given on pattern sheet 21.

This lightweight jacket will team well with all your skirts and pants. It is single-breasted and has a deep yoke. It also features buttoned sleeve bands and a tie belt that emerges from the side seams.

This attractive and up-to-date summer coat is made from the same pattern as the shorter jacket. It has raglan sleeves, a deep yoke at the back and front, patch pockets with top-stitched bands, buttoned sleeve bands, and a collar with a stand. And why not try making it up in a waterproofed fabric – the design makes a stylish and practical raincoat!

Making a collar with a stand

It is important to know how to make up and attach a collar with a stand which is stitched on. This technique is necessary when making jackets and coats which need a collar that fits well and looks smart. The stand is inserted far enough into the collar so that it supports and shapes the collar around the neck. You will find the seamline is invisible and the results well worth the extra effort.

■ Dark green = upper collar
■ Light green = under collar

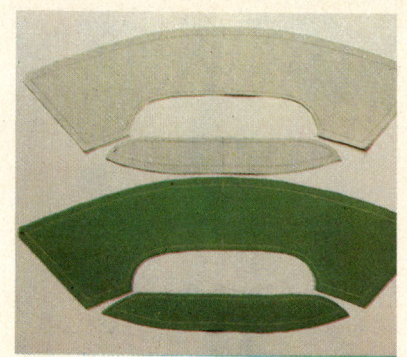

1 In the photograph above you can see all the pattern pieces cut out and ready for assembly. All of the collar pieces are cut from single fabric, and then the under collar and under collar stand are reinforced with iron-on interfacing to give extra support to the finished collar. Allow a seam allowance of 0.5 cm ($\frac{3}{16}$″) on seams of inner curve of the collar and the outer curve of the collar stand. Add 1 cm ($\frac{3}{8}$″) on all other edges.

2 Iron the interfacing onto the relevant pieces and then pin the under collar stand to the under collar, right sides facing. Baste and then stitch them together, then clip into the seam allowance around the curve several times close to the stitching line. Press the seam open. Now stitch the neckband to the upper collar in the same way. Pin and stitch under and upper collar together around outer edges, right sides facing. Turn and press.

3 Baste the two parts of the collar together along the stand seamline, wrong sides facing, and then top-stitch close to the stitching on both sides of the seam as shown above. Carefully pull out basting threads. Now baste together the upper and under collar edges that will be attached to the finished garment along the marked seamline. Top-stitch around the outer edges, following the directions for the required distance from edge.

4 On the right you see the finished collar. Note how the inserted collar stand allows the collar to shape and curve naturally around the neck without creasing or straining.

Now baste the collar to the neck edge. If using a pattern with a cut-in-one or attached facing, the collar is stitched between the garment and the facing.

If the garment is unlined, a back facing piece is usually included. In this case, stitch the shoulder seams of the front and back facing and finish the seam allowance of the outer edges. Pin the facing to the neck edge, right sides facing, placing the collar between the garment and the facing, and then stitch all around neck edge in one long seam.

5 Trim the seam allowances around the neck edge to 0.5 cm ($\frac{3}{16}$"), and then clip into the curve close to the stitching line.

Turn the facing to the inside of the garment and baste through all layers close to the seamline. Press the seam lightly on the inside of the garment, pull out all the basting threads, and press once more. Finally, sew the facing to the shoulder by hand. Make a few stitches which are firm, but not too tight, so that the shoulders do not wrinkle.

6 This detail shows the collar as it should look when the garment is completed. The collar, stitched between the garment and the facing, emerges neatly and smoothly from the neck seamline.

Zip-up raincoats in coated fabrics

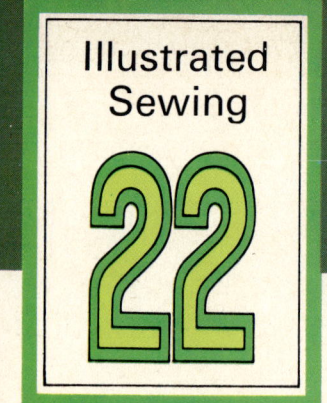

Illustrated Sewing 22

Fabrics with a plastic coating are ideal for everyday coats, especially for children as they are both tough and waterproof. Made in sizes R to V.

The yoke, sleeves, and two patch pockets are in plain-colored fabric to contrast with the multi-colored checks of the main fabric.

The pockets, sleeves, and shoulders have a buttoned-strap trim – another neat and decorative touch.

These coats are ideal for rainy weather. This style is exactly the same as the first style except for the addition of tiny cap sleeves or wings on the shoulders — another appealing design feature.

Working with coated fabrics

Plastic-coated fabrics are particularly suitable for children's wear. One side is treated with a plastic finish and the other side is untreated fabric. They are water-repellent and easy to keep clean. However, they can be a little difficult to sew sometimes and you will need some hints for stitching successfully. Perhaps the most important factor to remember is that mistakes are virtually irreparable. Once the fabric is stitched, alterations cannot be made. Removed stitches leave holes and there is nothing you can do about them. It is therefore worth making up the pattern in muslin first, so that necessary adjustments to the pattern can be made before cutting.

✸ Cut the pattern pieces from single fabric only. You will find that if the fabric is doubled and the smooth sides face each other, the fabric can shift about. Mark outlines with tailor's chalk.

✸ When stitching, use polyester thread if possible. When stitching seams with the right sides facing, be careful that the pieces don't shift. When stitching on the plastic side, oil the presser foot lightly to prevent it sticking.

✸ Make a test pressing on a scrap of the fabric. The fabric should be very damp (not dripping) and a damp cloth must always be used when pressing the treated surface, otherwise it could melt and stick to the iron. You will find that the color changes during pressing, but this will soon disappear when it dries. Since pressing does not ensure flat seams with this type of fabric, it is important to know how to make flat seams – see steps 1–2.

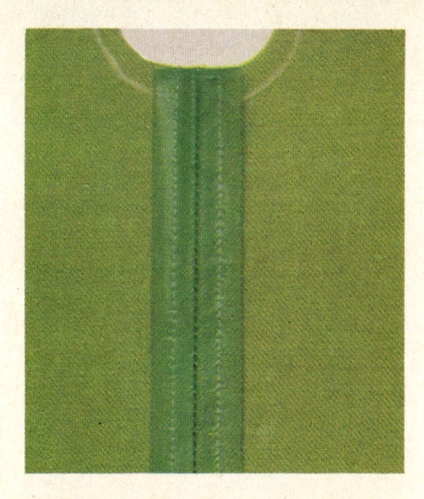

1 Having stitched the seam in the usual way, turn to the wrong side and stitch down the seam allowances, making the stitching lines equidistant from the seam. You do not need to finish the seam allowance because this type of fabric does not fray.

2 Here is another method for flattening seams successfully. Press strips of iron-on bonding net or a double-sided adhesive fabric between the fabric and the seam allowances. Be sure that the bonding fabric is washable.
Cut the strips to size, so that they do not protrude beyond the seam allowances or they are likely to stick to the iron when pressed. Place a damp cloth over the seam and press for 10–15 seconds. Leave to cool.
This method is quick and easy, but the seam allowances will show on the right side after pressing.

3 Sleeve seams are always difficult to reach, and particularly so on children's clothes. It is advisable to trim the seam allowance to 0.5 cm ($\frac{1}{4}''$) and press in one direction only.

Inserting an open-ended zipper

Open-end zippers are often used on sportswear and children's clothes. They are quick and easy to open and close and generally more versatile than the closed-end skirt or dress zipper.

First method

This is the simplest method of inserting the zipper. The front facing is cut-in-one with the garment and the zipper is stitched along the fold of the front edges.

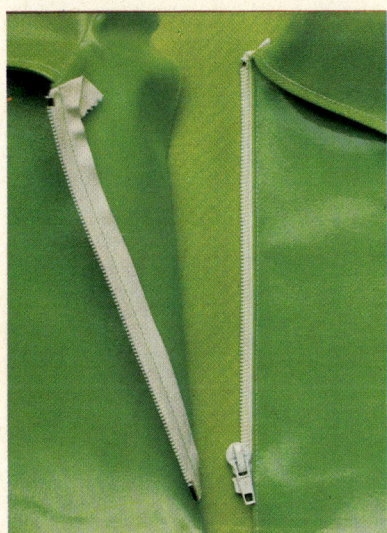

1 Open the zipper into two separate parts and then place the zipper tape under the edge so that the fold is right up against the teeth. Turn the upper edges of the tapes to the inside. Top-stitch close to the folds of the front edges. Using this method means that if the zipper is damaged, it is easy to replace. In the photograph above you can see the zipper opened up to show the inside of the garment too. Do not use pins because they will mark the fabric. Simply work slowly and carefully, holding the pieces firmly.

Second method

This method is used when the facing is cut as a separate piece. The zipper can be inserted between the fabric and the facing so that the tapes are not visible.

1 If the style has a collar pin the finished collar to the neck edge, pinning through the seam allowance only so that you don't mark the fabric. Turn under the front seam allowance on the edge of the facing and pin right sides together around the neck edge. Do not turn under the facing allowance on the front of the garment. Stitch around the neck edge, stitching through all layers.

2 The zipper is now stitched to the facing only. Open the zipper and place it under the pressed-down seam allowance of the facing so that the fold of the facing lies close to the teeth and the tape is hidden beneath the seam allowance. Turn back the upper ends of the tape and then top-stitch close to the folded edge.

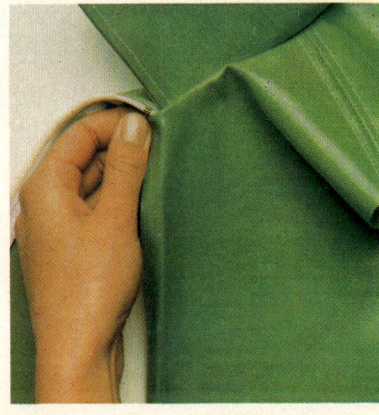

3 On the neck edge, turn the seam allowance of the garment front to the inside so that the seam allowances of the collar and the neck edge are covered.

4 Turn the seam allowance on the front edge under. Place this folded edge over the zipper tape which is stitched to the facing. Top-stitch close to the edge through all layers.

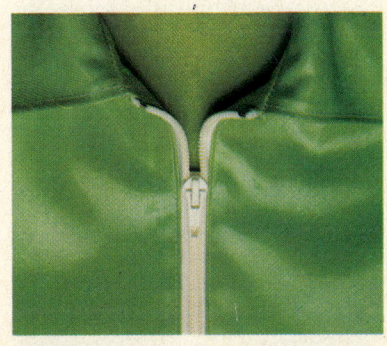

5 Here is the completed zipper. The zipper lies between the front and the facing and the zipper tape is invisible from the right side. This method gives a slightly neater finish.

Two skirts for everyday wear

Illustrated Sewing 23

This smart and attractive-looking skirt has been made up in a popular tartan. The pattern for this useful addition to your wardrobe is given on the pattern sheet in sizes D and F. The top-stitched pleats, released at hip level, have a particularly slimming effect, and practical pockets have been inserted into the pleat seams.

Making up the skirt in a plain fabric shows the pleats and the top-stitching to their best advantage. The detail shows the pockets inserted into the pleats. Note that the pleat down the center front is particularly flattering to the fuller figure.

A pocket in a knife pleat

It is a fairly simple matter to insert a pocket into the seam of a knife or side pleat. Two linings are required for each pocket. For heavy fabrics use a special pocket-lining fabric or taffeta; if the skirt is made up in a lightweight fabric, use same fabric.

1 Mark the pleat placement line and the pleat fold line, the marks indicating pocket placement, and the ends of the pleat stitching lines with basting. Finish the raw edges of the two pocket linings with machine zigzag stitching, before beginning to work them into the pleat seam. Then stitch one half to the center front, right sides facing, and the second half to the side front, extending the stitching beyond the seam allowances in both cases. Finish skirt edges together with the pockets, then press pockets as shown.

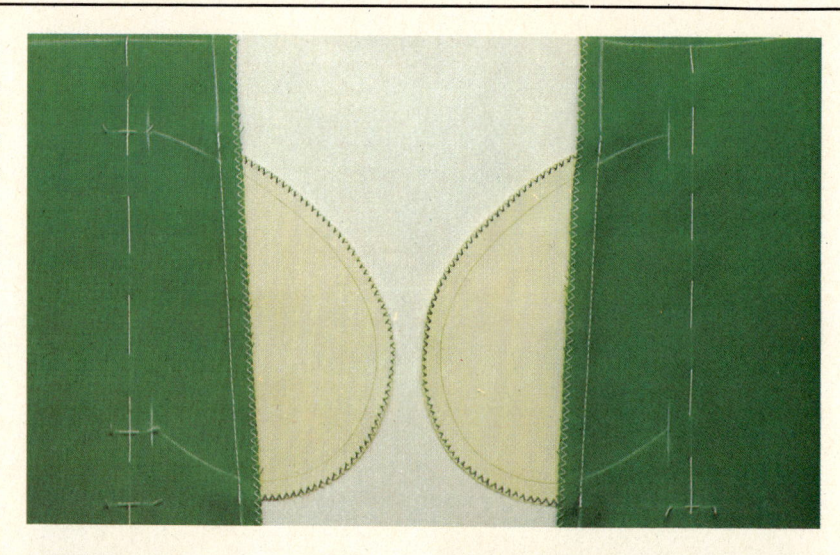

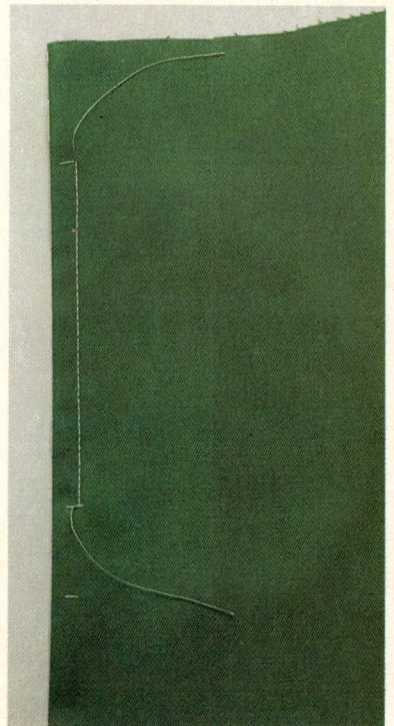

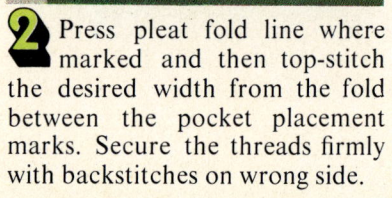

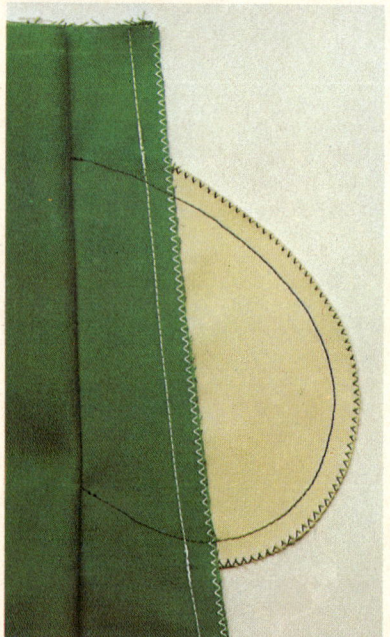

2 Press pleat fold line where marked and then top-stitch the desired width from the fold between the pocket placement marks. Secure the threads firmly with backstitches on wrong side.

3 Pin the pocket lining and the inner pleat seam together. When stitching the skirt and linings together, begin at the pocket marks and stitch across the inside of the pleat to meet the pocket lining. Now stitch the linings together in a gentle curve as shown in the photograph above.

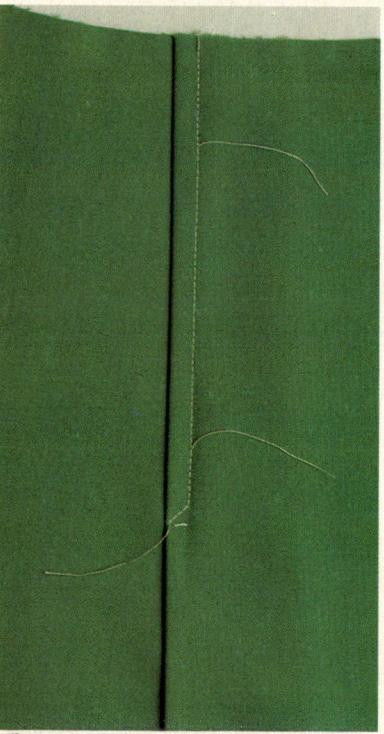

4 Turn to right side of garment and finish top-stitching pleat through all layers of fabric, angling across to the fold at the end. Secure and sew in ends on inside.

Working a box pleat

Below, we show the ever-popular box pleat. In this type of pleat, the two fold lines meet on the surface of the garment exactly over the center of the pleat underlap. The inner seams of this type of pleat are pressed to each side.

1 In the photograph on the right you can see the various pieces that make up the box pleat laid out for easy identification. On the right and left are the two skirt pieces with the pleat fold lines, the markings for the ends of the pleat stitching, lines, and the underlap placement all marked. The width of the pleat underlap (center) is the same as the two pleat extensions which are cut-in-one with the skirt pieces. Check that the ends of the pleat stitching lines marked on the fold lines meet at the same level.

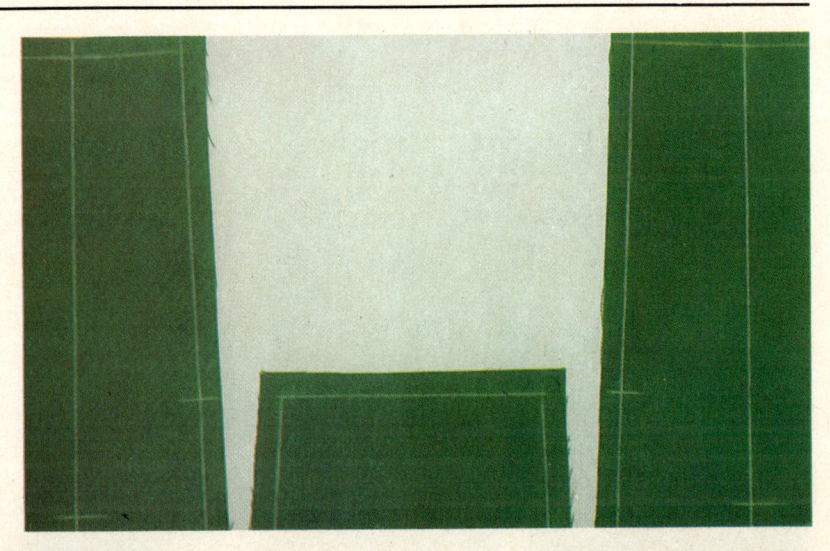

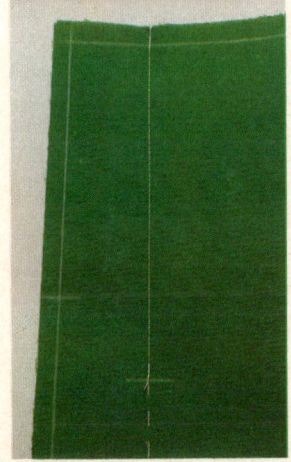

2 Pin the skirt pieces together, right sides facing, and then stitch along the marked pleat line as far as the cross markings on the pleat fold line, as shown above. Baste the remainder of this seam, working the hem as shown in Illustrated Sewing 9, photograph 3. Finally, carefully press this seam open.

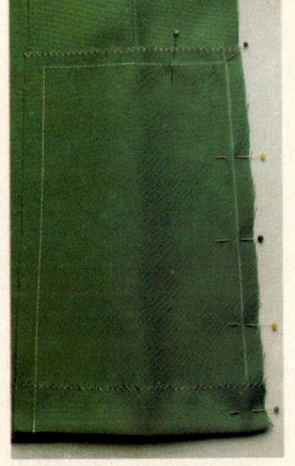

3 Finish the upper edge of the pleat underlap and stitch the hem. Pin the underlap into place so that the upper corners and the marks correspond. Stitch the underlap in place, stitching from the hem to the top of the underlap on each half. Stitch through the pleat and underlap only. Secure threads.

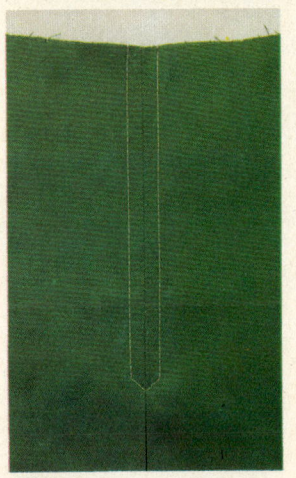

4 For a decorative effect, you can top-stitch the pleats down to the point at which the fulness is released. Either use the presser foot of your machine as a guide or mark the width with tailor's chalk or basting. Top-stitch with ordinary sewing thread, or use a twisted thread with ordinary thread wound onto the bobbin.

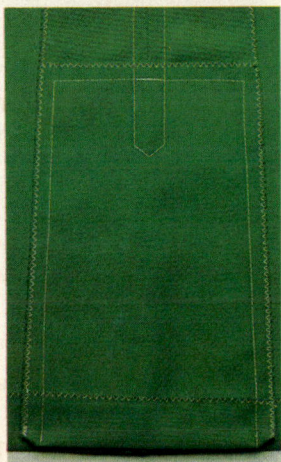

5 Before finishing the seam allowances together, turn under the corners of the underlap at the hem with small stitches worked by hand. These ensure that the hem of the pleat will not be visible from the right side of the garment. Above, you can see the completed box pleat from the wrong side. Press carefully.

Keep him in check

Illustrated Sewing 24

The wide shoulder yoke is cut on the bias of the check for decorative effect. The small buttoned strap adds an unusual touch.

These sporty shirts are given in sizes K and M on the pattern sheet (sizes J, L, and N can be adapted from the pattern sheet). Made in a soft cotton, the style is slightly waisted and has large, buttoned, patch pockets.

This shirt is exactly the same pattern as for the red checked shirt, but the effect is different. The back yoke is narrower, it has shoulder tabs and pocket flaps which are cut on the bias, and each pocket has a small inverted pleat down the center. These shirts have a genuine country look.

Patch pocket with inverted box pleat

The patch pocket is the easiest type of pocket to work. This style has an inverted box pleat down the center and a shaped pocket flap.

1 Transfer all the markings from your pattern onto the fabric. Mark the center with basting stitches as shown.

2 Fold the pocket, wrong sides facing, and stitch carefully from top to bottom along the pleat stitching line.

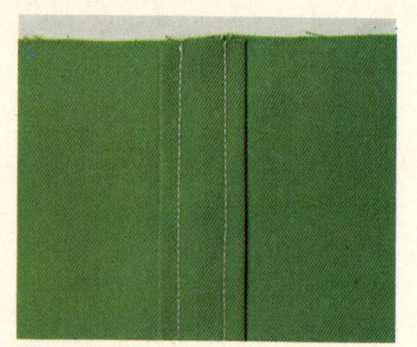

3 Press the pleat so that the basting lies down the center, directly above the stitching line. Top-stitch pleat along both folds.

Finish all raw edges except the top edge with machine zigzag stitching, then press under all the finished seam allowances. Turn under the top edge twice and stitch. With right sides facing, stitch the pocket flap pieces together around both short edge and the shaped long edge, then turn and top-stitch.

If you intend to top-stitch the pocket flap along the top edge from the right side as shown in photograph 5 below, you do not need to finish the top raw edges. However, if you are not going to top-stitch this edge, you must always finish these raw edges before stitching on the flap.

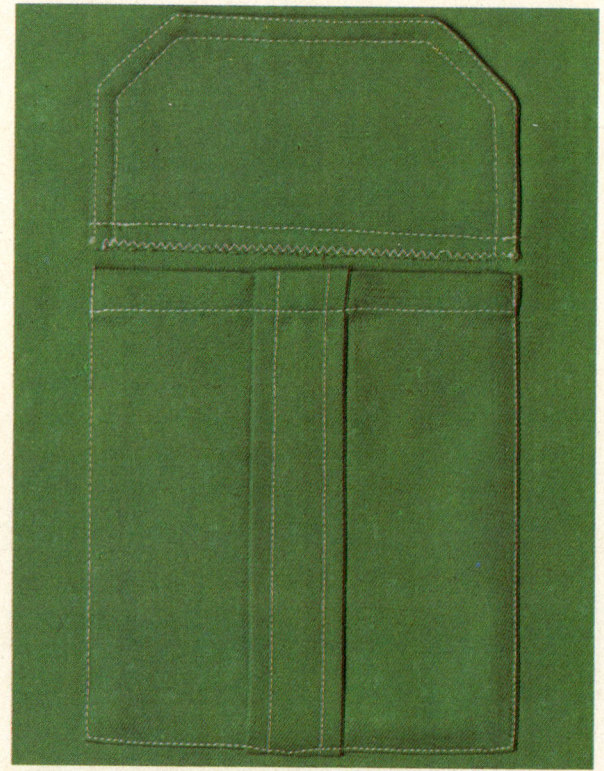

4 Baste the pocket where marked and stitch in place. Stitch flap 0.75 cm ($\frac{1}{4}''$) above pocket.

5 Work a vertical machine-stitched buttonhole in the center of the flap. Sew on the button.

Man's shirt sleeve slit opening

On a man's shirt, the lower sleeve width is drawn up in a pleat. A slit opening is worked with a buttonhole in the overlap. The cuff ends at the slit edges.

1 Transfer the slit opening marks to the fabric with tailor's chalk. Cut a piece of fabric for the overlap 6 cm (2½") wide by 2 cm (¾") longer than the length of the slit plus 1 cm (⅜") seam allowance all around. Press the strip in half lengthwise; press under seam allowances on upper edge, right edge for left sleeve, and left edge for right sleeve.

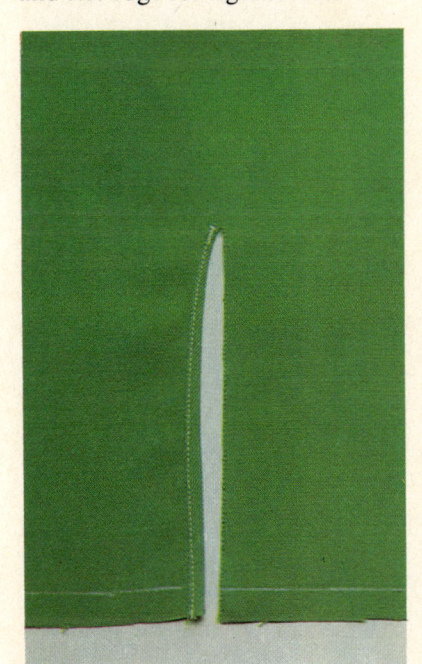

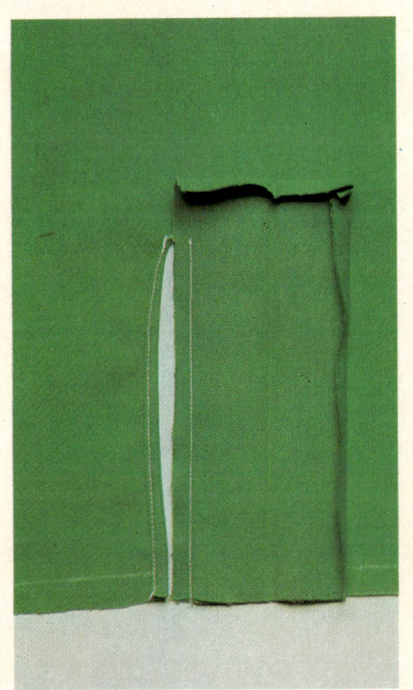

3 Pin unpressed edge of overlap to the raw edge of slit opening. The overlap seam allowance is 1 cm (⅜"), but leave only 0.5 cm (¼") on shirt edge. Stitch.

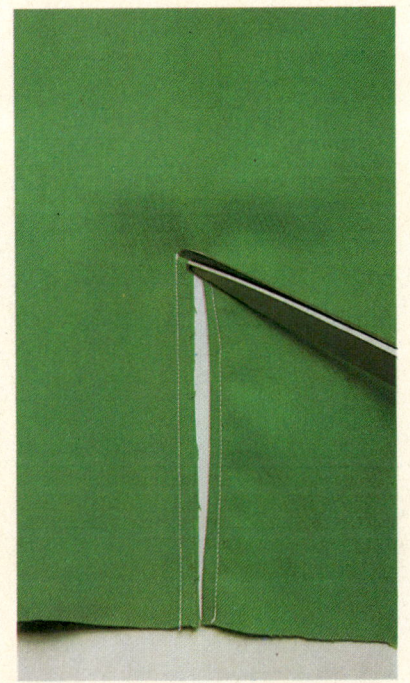

4 Working from the right side, clip into the corner of the overlap seam allowance, cutting diagonally as far as the stitching line. Do not cut through stitching.

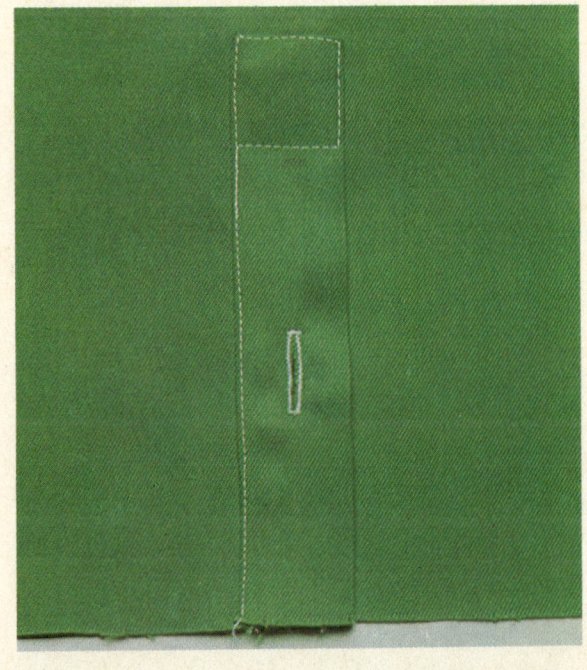

2 Cut the slit open carefully as far as the end marking. Turn under the underlap side narrowly twice, tapering at the top end. Stitch close to the edge and secure the ends firmly.

5 Turn overlap strip to right side. Turn under seam allowance and lay edge slightly over the stitching line. Baste in place. Top-stitch the overlap, making a square at top edge as shown. It is quite usual to add a buttoned fastening to the slit on a man's shirt sleeve. Mark the center as shown on the left and work a buttonhole. Sew on a button.

715

Cool and casual kimonos

If you are a beginner at sewing, a lightweight kimono is an ideal first project. Start work on it in the morning and you'll be able to wear your finished garment to watch television the very same evening. That's how quick and easy our pattern is. We give one basic shape for adults and one for children, but the shape is wide enough to fit most figures by merely tightening or loosening the belt.

Materials Required:
Woman: Styles with or without shoulder seams: Fabric: 3.80 m (4$\frac{1}{8}$ yds), 90 cm (36") wide. (Cut from folded fabric.)
Man: Styles with or without shoulder seams: Fabric: 3.50 m (3$\frac{7}{8}$ yds), 90 cm (36") wide. (Cut from folded fabric.)
Child: Style without shoulder seams: Fabric: 1.50 m (1$\frac{5}{8}$ yds), 90 cm (36") wide. Style with shoulder seams: Fabric: 1.45 m (1$\frac{5}{8}$ yds), 90 cm (36") wide. (Cut from single layer of fabric.)
Cutting out: Enlarge the pattern according to the diagram overleaf. The man's kimono is 17 cm (6$\frac{3}{4}$") shorter than the woman's.
Seam allowances: Add 1 cm ($\frac{3}{8}$") to all edges except front straight edge which has 2 cm ($\frac{3}{4}$") seam allowance. For hem, add 3 cm (1$\frac{1}{4}$") for adults, 5–8 cm (2"–3") for children to allow for growing.

Check the correct length before cutting out. The pattern pieces are straight-sided so they can be placed side by side on the fabric and cut out without wastage.
Front and back can be cut out in one piece without a shoulder seam, but with a seam at center back.

◀ She wears her lightweight kimono floor length. It is so wide and loose-fitting, that it suits all types of figure.

A kimono is ▶ perfect to show off a pretty fabric. Pick a fun print like the ones we have chosen, or splash out with a bold, exotic pattern.

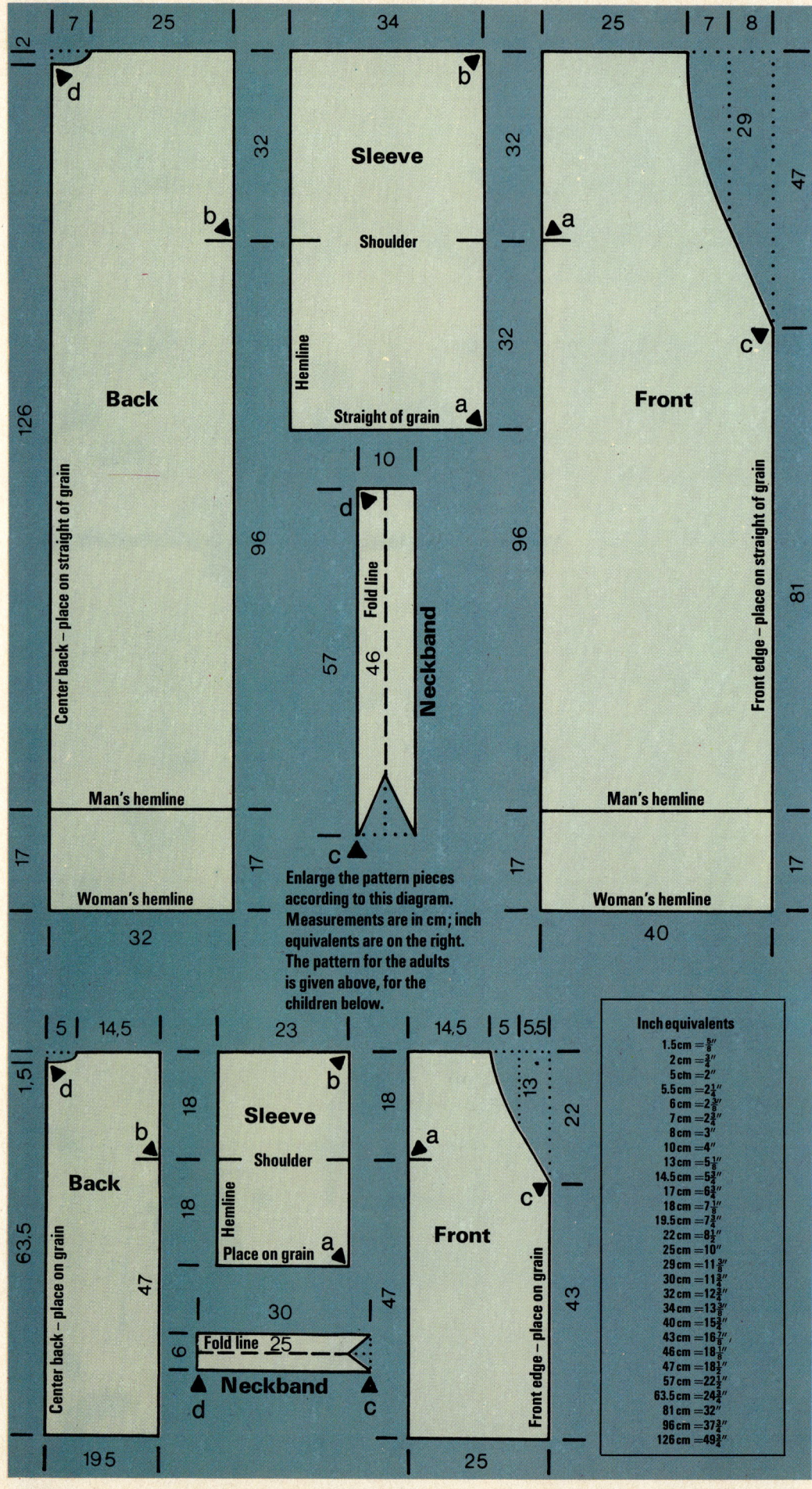

However, with a one-way design, a shoulder seam will be required, but no seam at center back.

Cut out the neckband twice on the fold. Tie belt for adults: Cut 2 strips each 130 cm (51") long and 8 cm (3") wide. Tie belt for children: Cut 2 strips 60 cm (23½") long, 6 cm (2¼") wide.

Sewing the kimonos

Join either center back or shoulder seams. Press seams to one side and finish raw edges together. Top-stitch through all thicknesses of fabric the presser foot width away from seamline.

Join side seams by matching point **a** on front to point **b** on back and stitching from hem to this point. Join sleeve seams (narrow sides), press to one side, and finish raw edges together. Turn under sleeve hem 1.5 cm (⅝") twice and stitch down. Pin and stitch in sleeve, matching points **a** and **b**. Finish edges together and press toward front or back.

Finish edges of side seams separately and press open. Turn under hem twice and stitch.

Join center back seam of neckband. Stitch together lower diagonal edges, right sides facing, up to seam allowance. Turn and press lengthwise along center.

Stitch 1 long side of neckband around neck opening, right side facing wrong side of kimono. Turn under seam allowance at other edge of neckband, bring it over to right side of kimono, and stitch close to neck edge.

Stitch the 2 parts of tie belt together. Fold belt in half lengthwise, right sides facing, and stitch, leaving an opening for turning. Turn belt to right side and press. Sew opening closed with slip stitches.

Sewing

In striped and checked cotton Practical kitchen cover-ups

The classic kitchen apron is back again. Prettier than an overall, but more practical than a frilly cocktail apron, the basic style can be adapted in different ways with trimmings such as braid, rickrack, lace, or bias strips.

The apron on the left is trimmed with scalloped braid, the one on the right with inserts of lace.

FOR ALL APRONS

Cutting out: Enlarge pieces to measurements given on the pattern. Add seam allowances. Skirt: waist 1 cm ($\frac{3}{8}$"), sides and hem 2 cm ($\frac{3}{4}$"). Pocket and bib: 1 cm ($\frac{3}{8}$") unless otherwise instructed. Waistband: 2 strips 4 cm ($1\frac{1}{2}$") wide, 150 cm (60") long with 1 cm ($\frac{3}{8}$") seam allowance all around. Straps: 2 strips 8 cm (3") wide, 100 cm ($39\frac{1}{2}$") long with 1 cm ($\frac{3}{8}$") seam allowance all around.

Sewing: Unless otherwise instructed, turn under hem twice and stitch. Make pleats at waist and tack. Fold and press shoulder straps lengthwise with seam allowances to inside. Stitch, catching in bib. Press under seam allowances on waistband strips. Stitch together, catching in skirt and bib. Stitch on pockets. Shoulder straps are crossed at back; work buttonholes in waistband and sew buttons to straps.

Style 1

Materials Required: Fabric: 2.50 m ($2\frac{3}{4}$ yds), 90 cm (36") wide. Cotton braid: 3.10 m ($3\frac{3}{8}$ yds).

For hem band, cut a strip 8 cm (3") wide with a 1 cm ($\frac{3}{8}$") seam allowance; turn under the 2 long edges. Stitch braid to both edges. Turn lower seam allowance of skirt to right side. Stitch band over skirt matching the checks carefully.

For bands for pockets and bib: cut 2 strips 4 cm ($1\frac{1}{2}$") wide, 17 cm ($6\frac{3}{4}$") long and 1 strip 4 cm ($1\frac{1}{2}$") wide, 22 cm ($8\frac{5}{8}$") long plus seam allowances. Attach in same way.

Style 2

Materials Required: Fabric: 2.50 m ($2\frac{3}{4}$ yds), 90 cm (36") wide. Insertion lace: 2.40 m ($2\frac{5}{8}$ yds).

Insert lace. In skirt: 1st row 8 cm (3") from edge, 2nd row 6.5 cm ($2\frac{1}{2}$") away. In bib: 1st row 2 cm ($\frac{3}{4}$") from upper edge, 2nd row 2 cm ($\frac{3}{4}$") away. In pockets: 1 row 4 cm ($1\frac{1}{2}$") from edge.

Style 3

Materials Required: Fabric: 2.50 m ($2\frac{3}{4}$ yds), 90 cm (36") wide. Cotton lace: 1.20 m ($1\frac{3}{8}$ yds).

Add 2 cm ($\frac{3}{4}$") to upper edge of bib when cutting out. Turn under twice and stitch. Stitch on lace border 3 cm ($1\frac{1}{4}$") from upper edge. At hem, stitch on lace 10 cm (4") from edge.

Style 4

Materials Required: Fabric: 1.90 m ($2\frac{1}{8}$ yds), 140 cm (54") wide.

Hem band, pockets, and bib are all cut on the bias

In the same basic pattern, this apron in butcher boy stripes is trimmed with wide borders of white cotton lace.

On the blue checked apron, the pockets, bib, and hem are cut on the bias to give an interesting contrast.

with a 1 cm (3/8″) seam allowance. Stitch hem band on as for Style 1 (without the braid). Turn under upper edge of bib and pockets and stitch.

Style 5

Materials Required: Fabric: 2.50 m (2¾ yds), 90 cm (36″) wide. Trim: Remnant of white cotton.

Cut out the white bands on bib and pockets according to the diagram. Stitch right side of bands to wrong side of bib and pockets. Clip seam allowance and turn. Press seam allowance toward bands, then topstitch in place.

Style 6

Materials Required: Fabric: 2.50 m (2¾ yds), 90 cm (36″) wide. Rickrack:

Pattern for skirts: Numbers are centimeters, inch equivalents are: 68cm = 26¾″; 7 cm = 2¾″; 8 cm = 3″; 14 cm = 5½″; 17 cm = 6¾″; 11 cm = 4½″; 6cm = 2½″; 9 cm = 3½″; 21 cm = 8¼″; 10 cm = 4″; 8.5 cm = 3¼″; 5 cm = 2″; 19 cm = 7½″; 45 cm = 17¾″. Enlarge pattern pieces. Pocket and bib trims are for Style 5 only.

1.60 m (1¾ yds) each of red, white, and blue. Add 2 cm (¾″) to the upper edge of bib and pockets when cutting out. Turn under the upper edges twice and stitch. Stitch on the rickrack in parallel rows 2 cm (¾″) apart. At the hem, the 1st row is 8 cm (3″) from the edge, on the bib the 1st row is 2 cm (¾″) from the upper edge, and on the pockets 1st row is 1 cm (3/8″) from the upper edge.

Large pockets on an apron are very useful. Here the pockets and bib are trimmed with contrasting fabric.

Gingham checks are always fresh-looking. This apron is trimmed with rows of rickrack braid.

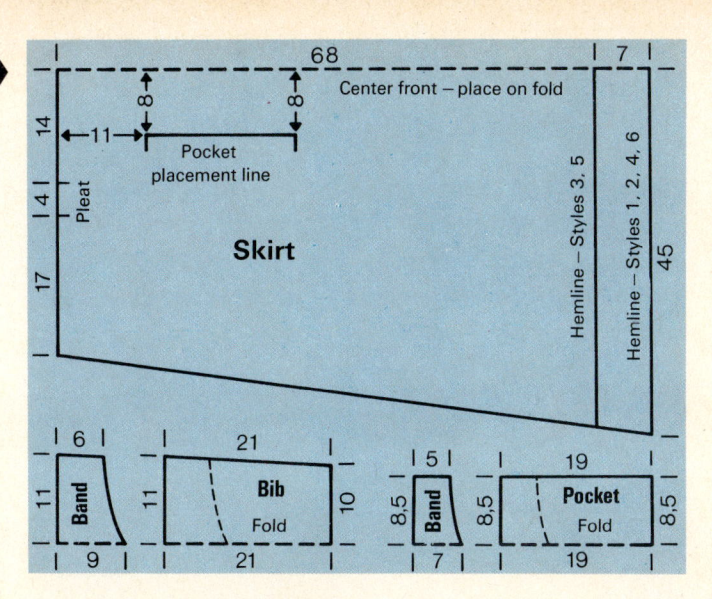

Quick to sew, comfortable to wear

Skirting's the issue

These skirts are softly flared and team up well with simple T-shirts and blouses. The pattern is a semi-circle with only one seam, so it's easy to draw the pattern — all you need is your waist measurement and skirt length. Three versions of the skirt are shown here. The one in the middle is quite plain — you just sew on the waistband and zipper. The one on the left has pockets with buttoned flaps, while the one on the right has patch pockets and ties at the waist.

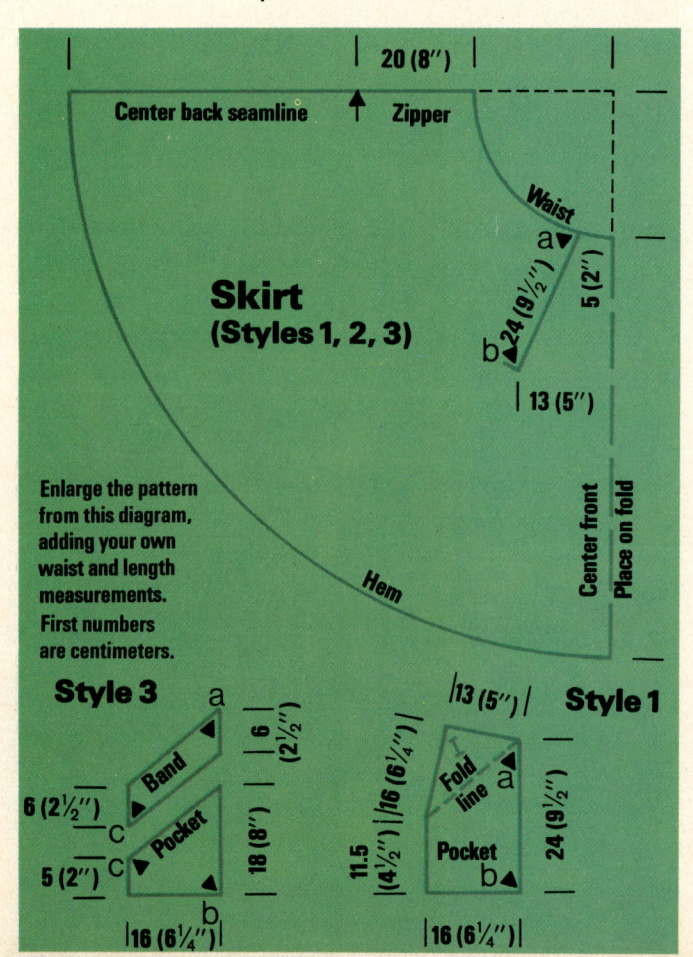

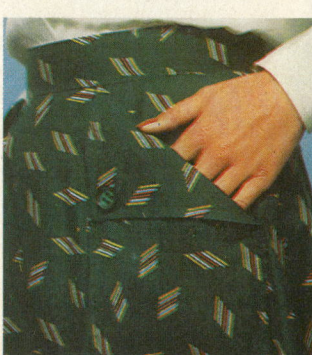

Enlarge the pattern from this diagram, adding your own waist and length measurements. First numbers are centimeters.

Style 1 has patch pockets with button-down flaps. Style 2 in the center is plain, while Style 3 has a bow tied at the waist and patch pockets. The simple style shows off interesting prints to advantage.

Style 1

Sewing

Cutting out
Fold fabric in half widthwise. Place pattern so center back is parallel to selvage and center front is on fold line. Add seam allowance of 2 cm ($\frac{3}{4}$"). Cut out. For waistband, cut strip 8 cm (3") wide by waist measurement, adding 6 cm ($2\frac{1}{2}$") for overlap and seam allowance.

Style 1: For each pocket, cut two pieces.

Style 3: For each pocket, cut one piece with band, one without, then cut one more band. For waist ties, cut 2 strips 8 cm (3") wide, 85 cm ($33\frac{1}{2}$") long, plus 3 cm ($1\frac{1}{4}$") seam allowance.

Making the skirt
Join center back seam to zipper opening. Finish seam allowances. Stitch in zipper. Press waistband in half lengthwise. Sew interfacing along fold line. Finish raw edge below interfacing. Stitch long edge of waistband without interfacing to skirt, right sides together, with 3 cm ($1\frac{1}{4}$") underlap at back. Turn waistband to inside. From right side, stitch along previous stitching line, catching in loops for hanging. Topstitch. Sew on skirt hook. Turn under 1 cm ($\frac{3}{8}$") twice for hem.

Style 1: Stitch pocket pieces together, right sides facing. Turn; press. Work buttonhole in flap. Stitch pockets to skirt. Sew on button, turn down flap.

Style 3: Stitch detached bands to pockets, right sides together. Stitch each cut-in-one pocket to a stitched pocket, right sides together. Turn; press. Topstitch around bands. Stitch pocket to skirt. Fold ties in half lengthwise, right sides facing, and stitch. Turn, press, and top-stitch. Stitch to sides of waistband.

Materials Required: (For sizes A to D) Cotton fabric: 2 m ($2\frac{1}{4}$ yds) 140 cm (54") wide. Skirt hook. Zipper: 20 cm (8"). Waistband interfacing. Thread.

Making the pattern
Draw an angle of 90° onto a large piece of tissue paper. Take your waist measurement, then multiply it by 7 and divide by 22. Mark this distance on both sides of the angle. Then draw a quarter circle by joining the 2 points. Determine the finished length of the skirt and mark this length on the angle in the same way, measuring from the waistband. Draw another curve at this distance, by connecting the 2 points.

To draw the curves, use a long piece of string with a pencil at one end. Hold the other end at the center of the angle.

Mark in the zipper opening at the center back and the positioning line for the pockets. Finally, draw the pattern pieces for the appropriate pockets if desired.

723

Sewing

A soft touch!

This casual little top is striking and different. Make it up in velour or stretch towelling, then trim the edges with bands of knitting in bright stripes.

Sewing

Here is the top made up in another color scheme. An attractive roll-away collar has been added to the neckband – very flattering and up-to-date!

Size: Directions are for 88 cm or 34½″ bust. Changes for 96 cm or 37½″ bust are in brackets.

Materials Required: Cotton velour or stretch towelling: 1.4 m (1½ yds), 86–90 cm (34–36″) wide. Elastic thread. Sewing thread.

50 gm or 2 oz each of 3 colors. Knitting needles size 1 (Am) or 12 (Eng).

Basic Pattern: K 1, P 1 rib.

Color Sequence: Orange model: Cast on and work 5 R orange, 6 R each blue and green.

Brown model: Cast on and work 5 R brown, 6 R each cream and red.

Note: When repeating the sequence, begin with 6 R orange or brown.

Tension: 25 sts and 48 R = 10 cm or 4″ with rib well stretched.

Abbreviations: K = knit. P = purl. St(s) = stitch(es).

Knitting the borders

Hip Border (make 2): Cast on 96 (102) sts in orange or brown and work Color Sequence 2 times in K 1, P 1 rib. Cast off loosely.

Sleeve Bands: Cast on 74 (80) sts and work as for Hip Border.

Neckband: Cast on 236 (250) sts in green or red. Work the Color Sequence 1 time in reverse. Work in rib, and K center 2 sts together in every 2nd R 8 times. Cast off remaining 220 (234) sts in rib.

Collar (make 2 pieces): Cast on 44 sts in red and work in rib, working the Color Sequence in reverse 5 times. Join the 2 parts together in the last brown row by grafting.

Cutting out the top

Enlarge the pattern pieces from the graph. Add 1.5 cm (⅝″) seam allowance on all seamlines.

Fold the fabric in half lengthwise. Place the pieces on the fabric so that the pile runs from top to bottom on all pieces.

Sewing the top

First, test the stitch tension and length on a scrap of fabric. (Note that pile fabrics are stitched in the direction of the pile.) Stitch the shoulder, side, and sleeve seams and then finish all raw edges neatly. Sew or stitch the knitted Hip Border and Sleeve Bands into circles, and then pin in position on the garment by stretching the knitting to the correct size. Stitch with elastic thread, by loading your sewing machine with thread on the top and elastic thread wound onto the bobbin. Sew on knitted Neckband. For Collar, place it under the Neckband and stitch to the neck edge. Fold the Collar back over the Neckband.

725

1 square = 3 cm (1¼")

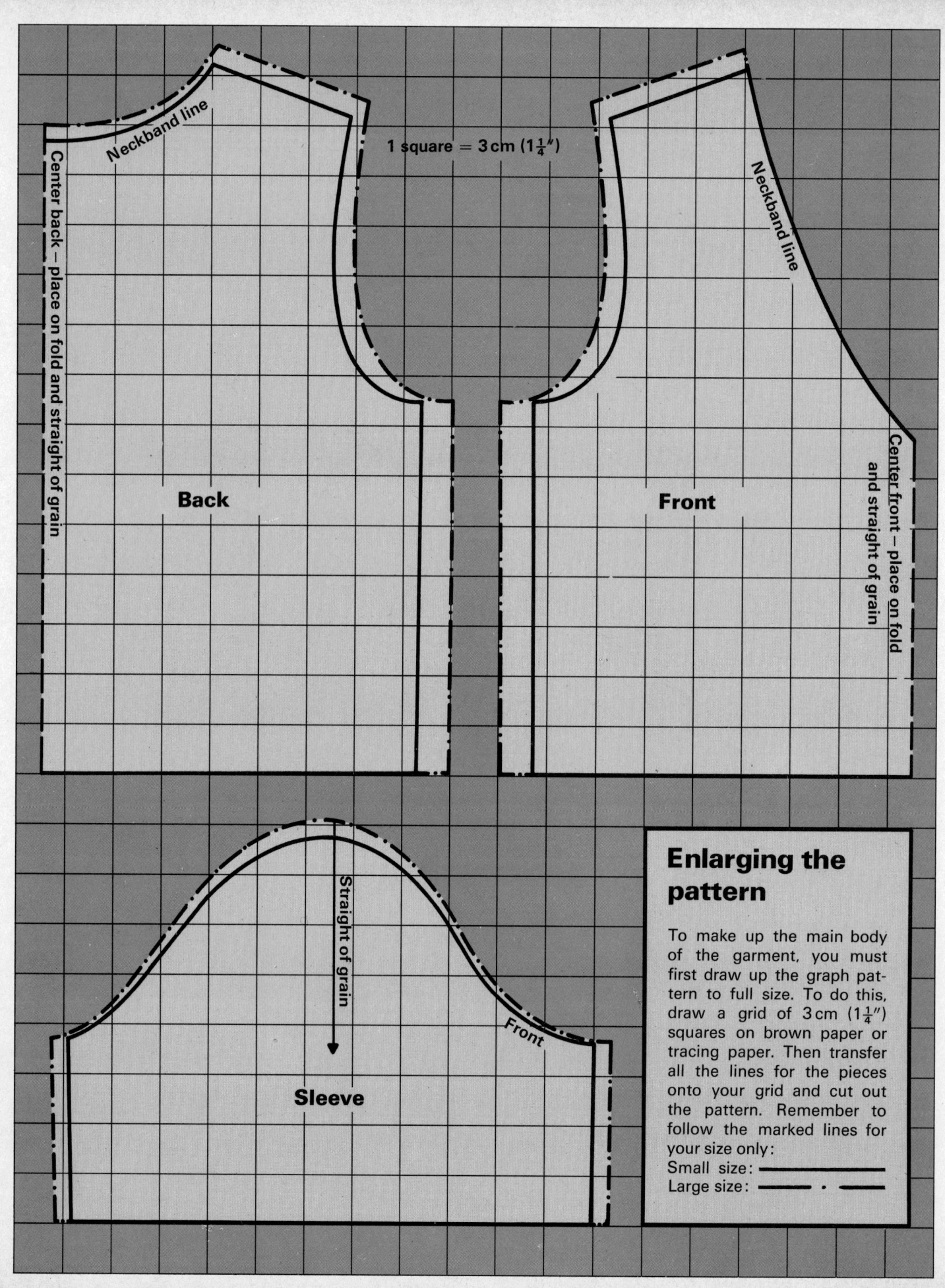

Neckband line

Center back – place on fold and straight of grain

Back

Neckband line

Center front – place on fold and straight of grain

Front

Straight of grain

Front

Sleeve

Enlarging the pattern

To make up the main body of the garment, you must first draw up the graph pattern to full size. To do this, draw a grid of 3 cm (1¼") squares on brown paper or tracing paper. Then transfer all the lines for the pieces onto your grid and cut out the pattern. Remember to follow the marked lines for your size only:
Small size: ⎯⎯⎯⎯
Large size: ⎯·⎯·⎯

Bedtime story

If you like to treat yourself to lazy weekends, our handy hold-all is just for you. It slots neatly in between the bedframe and the mattress and holds everything you need for a little self-indulgence!

Materials Required: Canvas: 0.90 m (1 yd), 150 cm (58") wide. 4 pieces of cardboard: For front 40.5 cm x 24.5 cm (16" x 9¾"); for flap 40.5 cm x 14 cm (16" x 5½"); for base 40.5 cm x 5.5 cm (16" x 2¼"); for back 40.5 cm x 25 cm (16" x 9⅞").

Cutting out: Draw the pattern pieces from the measurements on the diagram. Add 1 cm (⅜") all around for the seam allowance. Cut out bag and whole gusset twice, the patch pocket once.

Sewing: The bag is worked double. First, with right sides facing, stitch together the 2 side edges of the flap only down to the 4th stitching line (point **f**). Turn to the right side.

To make the patch pocket, fold where marked on the diagram and join the lengthwise seam. Press open the seam allowances and turn the pocket. Top-stitch close to the upper edge. Now baste the pocket to one layer of the bag front where marked and stitch along the vertical division lines. Then pin both front layers together, wrong sides facing, and stitch the patch pocket along its lower edge through all thicknesses.

Stitch through both bag layers along the 1st, 2nd, and 3rd stitching lines, leaving the sides open. Push in the cardboard for the base. Fold each gusset in half, wrong sides facing. Line up the cut edges and stitch to the front through all layers from **c** to **d**, right sides facing. Snip into the seam allowance of the front at the top corners. Join the gusset to the base from **d** to **e**, then stitch it to the back up to point **f**.

Push in the cardboard for the front and back. Stitch through both

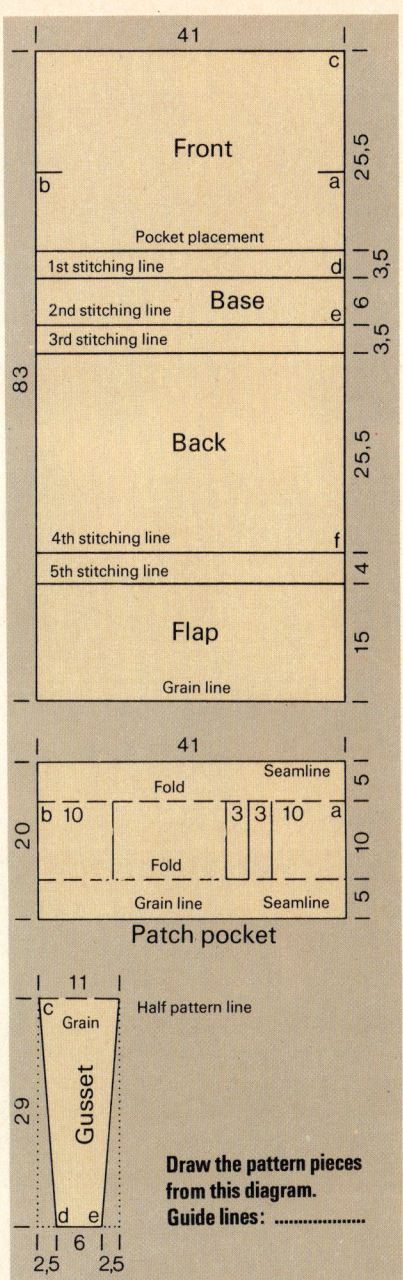

Inch equivalents:
2.5 cm = 1"; 3 cm = 1¼"; 3.5 cm = 1⅜"; 4 cm = 1½"; 5 cm = 2"; 6 cm = 2½"; 10 cm = 4"; 11 cm = 4½"; 15 cm = 6"; 20 cm = 8"; 25.5 cm = 10⅛"; 29 cm = 11⅜"; 41 cm = 16⅛"; 83 cm = 33".

1 The hold-all will take everything you need for a lazy morning in bed.
2 The pocket is divided up into several smaller compartments.
3 The flap is reinforced with cardboard and can be wedged in between the mattress and the bedframe.

thicknesses along the 4th and 5th stitching lines.

Turn in the seam allowance at the upper front and top-stitch close to edge. Insert cardboard into flap, turn in remaining seam allowances and stitch together close to edge.

Sewing

Lots of sewing ideas
Specially designed for baby

Here, and on the following pages are lots of pretty and practical items specially created with baby in mind. They are all easy to sew, economical, and would make wonderful presents for any new mother. In the photograph above, you can see how comfortable our baby looks in his bed lined with a well-padded surround to prevent him from hurting himself. The pillowcase and cover are made of towelling.

♥ DOLL

Height: 27 cm (10½″).
Materials Required:
Towelling. Remnants of yarn and decorative edging. Bias binding. Kapok for stuffing.

Cut out the doll's body twice in towelling and sew together, leaving an opening in the head. Turn and stuff with kapok. Sew up the opening by hand. Embroider eyes and a mouth with satin stitch. Sew a fringe of cotton yarn onto the head for hair. Make the little cap and bind with bias binding. Sew a length on either side for tying a bow. Stuff a little kapok into the back of the cap to make the head round. Place the cap on the head with the hair showing. Sew the cap in place.

Cut out the dress twice on the fold, then stitch the side seams. Sew hem, catching in edging under the hem. Dress the doll and sew shoulder seams.

♥ BALL

Materials Required:
Towelling. Kapok. Cut out the towelling segments 6 times with a 1 cm (⅜″) seam allowance. Stitch the segments together, leaving an opening in the center of last seam. Turn, stuff with kapok, sew up opening.

♥ PLAYSUIT

Materials Required: Soft towelling: 40 cm x 104 cm (15¾″ x 41″). Dotted cotton: 20 cm (¼ yd), 90 cm (36″) wide. Scrap of white cotton. A quarter of the playsuit is given on the graph pattern.

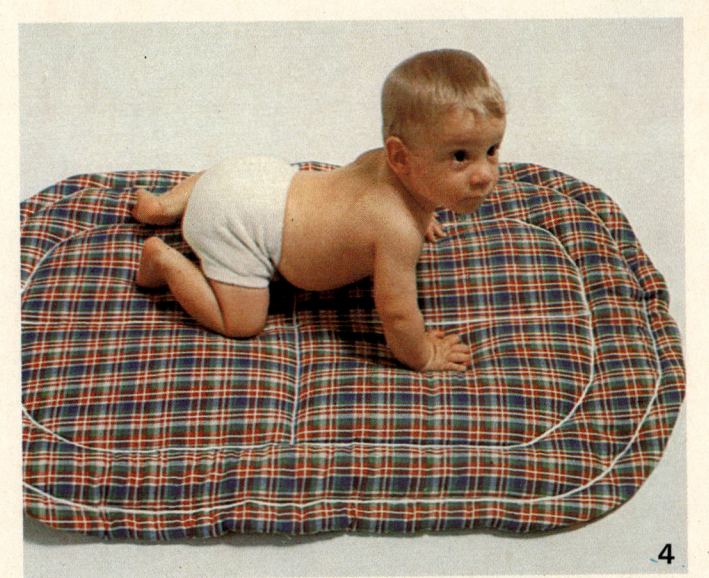

Trace the piece twice and tape together, adding 1 cm (⅜″) seam allowance at the sides. Cut the playsuit in one piece, placing the bottom on the fold.
Stitch the side seams and finish with zigzag stitching. Cut a 18 cm (7″) slit down the center back and bind this and the upper edge with the dotted cotton so that the finished width is 0.5 cm (¼″). At the left and right of the slit, sew two 5 cm (2″) loops for the ties. Cut 2 strips of dotted cotton 6 cm (2½″) wide by 65 cm (25½″) long plus seam allowance. Fold, stitch, and turn to make ties. Sew at the front 3 cm (1¼″) to the left and right of center. These are crossed over at the back, threaded

1 It's very important that your baby's toys are soft so that he cannot hurt himself. The little doll and the ball are made of towelling stuffed with kapok and are very huggable.

2 This roomy playsuit gives a baby plenty of kicking room, but is also nice and warm.

3 The shoulder straps, which are sewn to the front, are crossed at the back and tied into a bow.

4 A changing mat is indispensible for baby's comfort and yours. This mat is made of cotton, filled with a layer of batting or wadding and trimmed with braid to hold the layers together.

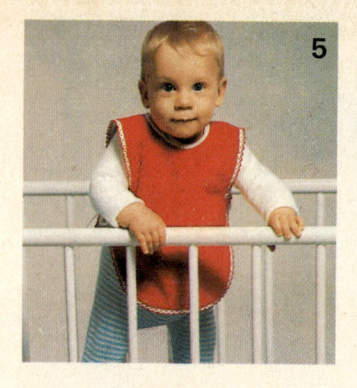

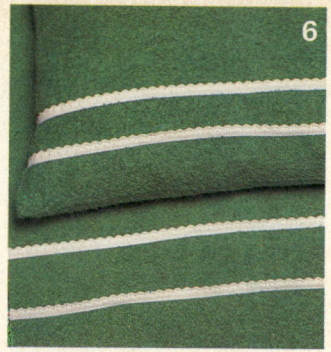

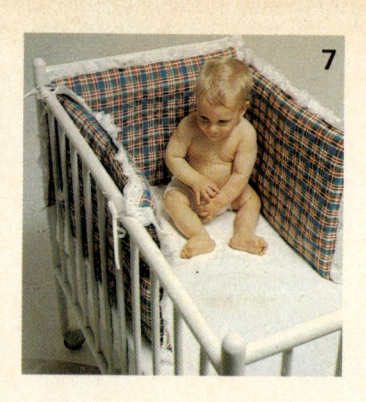

5 A large bib in towelling is very practical and can easily be washed in the washing machine.

6 An idea for baby's bed: Make covers from bright towelling trimmed with white braid.

7 The cot has a padded surround so that baby cannot knock himself against the sides. It consists of three separate cushions fastened to the rails with ties.

8 A night-time sleeping bag for sweet dreams. It is trimmed with a colorful braid border and has a zipper at the front.

9 This is a warm towel with a trimmed hood that you can wrap baby in after his bath.

through the loops, and tied in a bow. Finally, cut out the flower motif in dotted cotton, appliqué a circle in the center in white fabric, and stitch to the front of the playsuit with zigzag stitching.

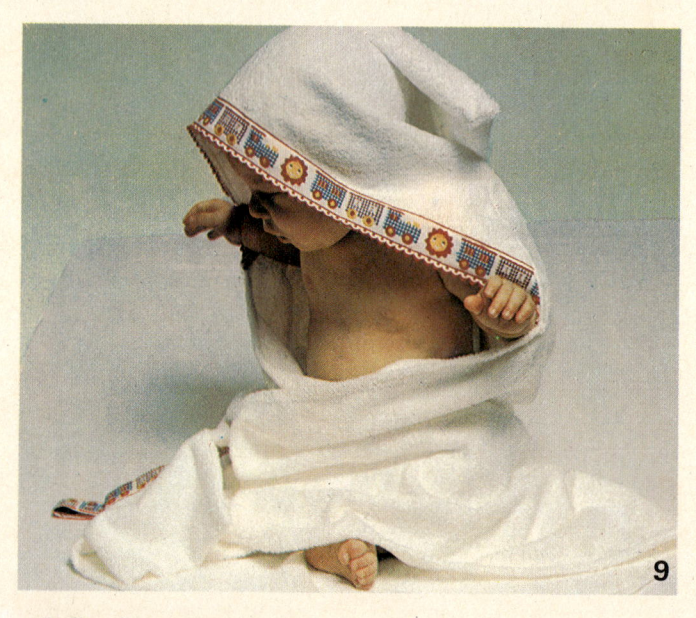

♥ CHANGING MAT

Size: 95 cm x 62 cm (37½" x 24½").

Materials Required:
Checked cotton fabric: 2 m (2¼ yds), 90 cm (36") wide. White cotton braid: 5.60 m (6⅛ yds), 0.5 cm (¼") wide. Batting or wadding for interlining: 0.65 m (¾ yd), 115 cm (45") wide (pieced if necessary).

A quarter of the mat is given on the graph pattern. Trace 4 times and tape together. Cut out the top and bottom of the mat with a 1 cm (⅜") seam allowance, the interlining without a seam allowance. Tack the interlining to the bottom piece of the mat. Stitch the top and bottom together, right sides facing, then turn to the right side. Finally, stitch the narrow braid to the top of the mat along the two oval lines marked on the pattern, through all layers. Stitch a cross inside the inner oval.

♥ BIB

Materials Required:
Towelling: 25 cm x 60 cm (10" x 23¾"). White bias binding: 0.50 m (½ yd). Decorative braid: 2 m (2¼ yds), 2 cm (¾") wide. Tape or ribbon for ties: 0.90 m (1 yd).

A quarter of the bib is given. Trace twice and tape together. Cut out on fold with 1 cm (⅜") seam allowance (neck edge has no seam allowance). At center back, cut a slit 10 cm (4") long; bind slit and neck edge with white bias binding. Finish seam allowances with zigzag stitching, then turn to inside and baste. Bind the outer edges of the bib with braid. Stitch a 22 cm (8½") length of tape onto each corner of armhole opening.

♥ DUVET AND PILLOW SET

Sizes: Duvet: 75 cm (29½") square. Pillow: 40 cm x 30 cm (15¾" x 11¾").

Materials Required: Soft towelling: 1.95 m (2⅛ yds), 90 cm (36") wide. Thick batting or wadding: 2.65 m (2⅞ yds), 90 cm (36") wide. Cotton: 1.80 m (2 yds), 90 cm (36") wide. Braid: 2.50 m (2¾ yds). Large flat press studs or snaps.

Note: This method of making covers can be adapted to any size by altering the measurements. For the duvet cover, cut

Enlarging the pattern pieces

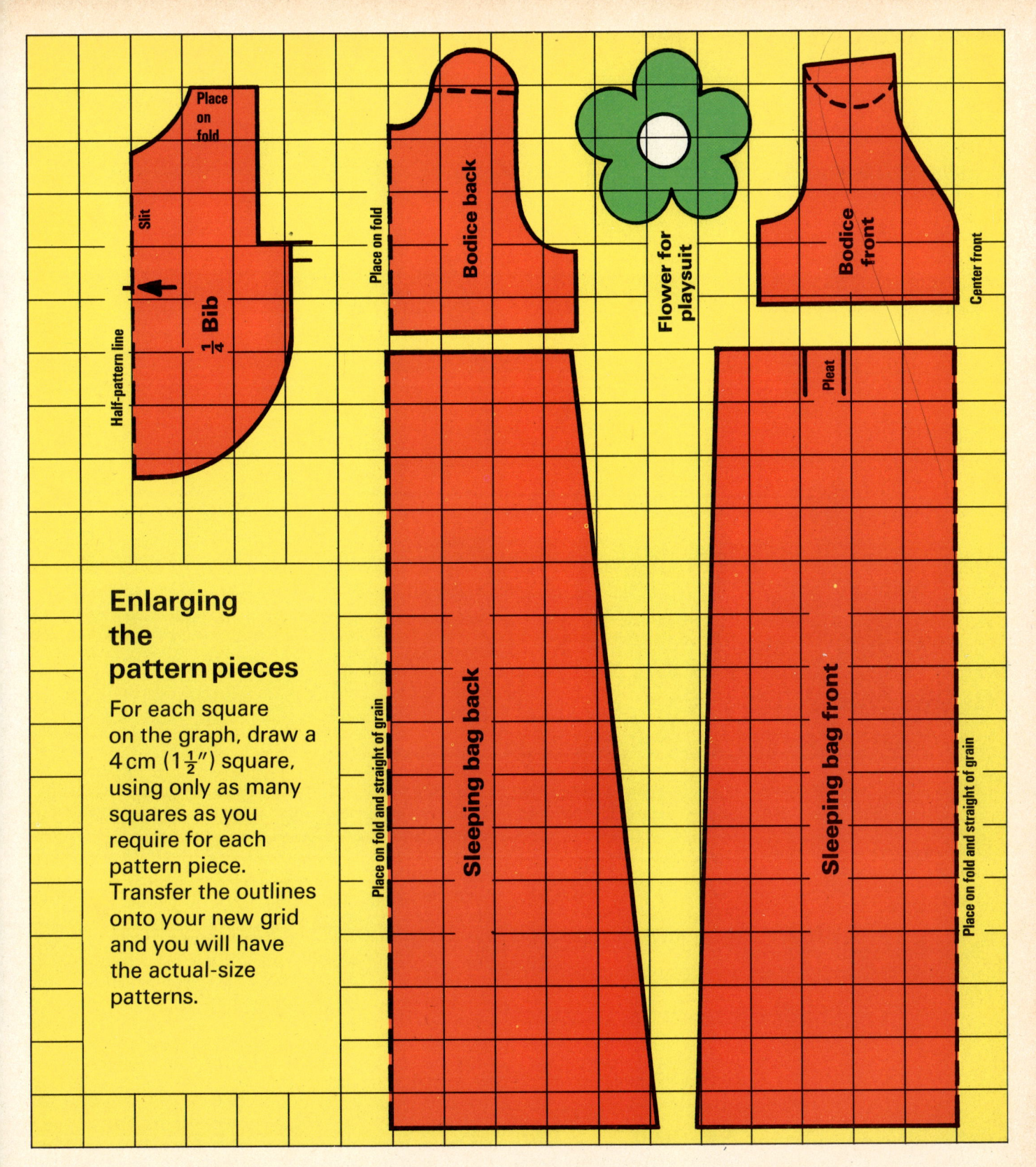

For each square on the graph, draw a 4 cm (1½") square, using only as many squares as you require for each pattern piece. Transfer the outlines onto your new grid and you will have the actual-size patterns.

a piece measuring 75 cm x 160 cm (29½" x 63") plus a 1 cm (⅜") seam allowance on the long sides. Make flat hems 3 cm (1¼") wide on the two narrow ends.
On one end of the cover, stitch two lines of braid 5 cm (2") apart and 10 cm (4") from the edge.
Fold the fabric, right sides facing, so that the side with the braid measures 75 cm (29½") and the other 79 cm (31"). Fold the extra 4 cm (1½") over the other edge (hem over hem) and pin down. Stitch both side seams and turn the cover to the right side. Sew large flat plastic studs or snaps in between the hems.
For pillow cover, cut a strip 30 cm x 90 cm (12" x 36") with a 1 cm (⅜") seam allowance on the long sides. Make the pillow cover in the same way as the duvet cover. The braid is sewn on 4 cm (1½") apart and the same distance from one long seam.
To make the pillow, cut 3 pieces of batting or wadding 40 cm x 30 cm (15¾" x 11¾") and overcast the

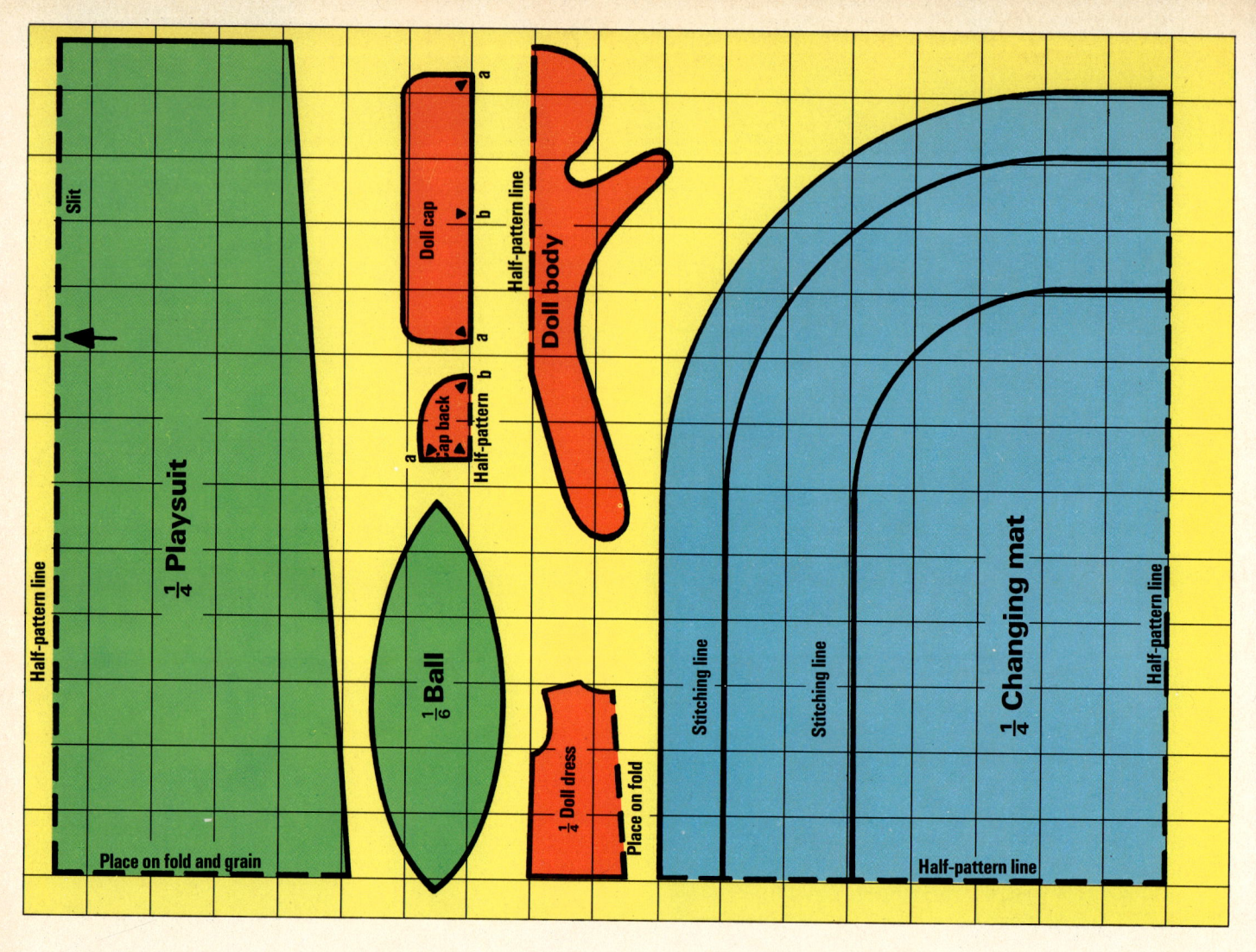

edges. Make an inner cover for the pillow from the cotton. Insert the pillow in the towelling cover. Make the duvet in the same way.

❤️ BED SURROUND
Size: Each panel is 37 cm x 55 cm (14⅝" x 21⅝").
Materials Required:
Checked cotton fabric: 1.60 m (1¾ yds), 90 cm (36") wide. Batting or wadding: 1 m (1⅛ yds), 90 cm (36") wide. Embroidered white edging: 4.80 m (5¼ yds). White tape or ribbon for ties: 2.40 m (2⅝ yds).
Cut out 2 pieces for each panel with 1 cm (⅜") seam allowance. Cut the filling without seam allowance. Stitch the panel pieces together with the slightly gathered edging stitched into 2 narrow and 1 long side. Turn and insert the filling. Fasten 2 pieces of tape 20 cm (8") long onto each upper corner.

❤️ PRINTED PILLOWCASE
(Photographs 2 and 3).
Size: 48 cm x 76 cm (19" x 30").
Materials Required:
Printed cotton: 1.10 m (1¾ yds), 90 cm (36") wide. Work in the same way as the green towelling duvet and pillow covers.

❤️ SLEEPING BAG
Materials Required: Soft towelling: 1.20 m (1⅜ yds), 90 cm (36") wide. Soft lining fabric: Same as for towelling. Children's braid: 0.65 m (¾ yd) long. White bias binding: 2.30 m (2½ yds). Zipper: 55 cm (22") long.
Cut out the sleeping bag back and front and the back bodice on the fold. Add 1.5 cm (⅝") seam allowance only to the side seams and the lower end. Place the wrong side of the pieces onto the lining fabric and cut out in the same way. Towelling and lining are worked as one. Stitch side seams and the bottom seam of the bag. Finish with zigzag stitching.
Then cut a 45 cm (17¾") slit in the front bag piece and bind with white bias binding. Join the bodice pieces at the side seams. Bind the sleeve, shoulder, and neck edges with bias binding. Place the rounded end of the back shoulder strap over the front shoulder strap, and stitch together along the curve.
Stitch the children's braid to the bodice, and then the bag, folding the front into pleats where indicated. Finally, stitch in the zipper.

❤️ BATH TOWEL WITH HOOD
Size: 95 cm (37½") square.
Materials Required:
Towelling: 1.60 m (1¾ yds), 115 cm (45") wide. Children's embroidered braid: 55 cm (22") long.
Cut out the 95 cm (37½") square towel with a 1 cm (⅜") seam allowance all around. Also cut out a right-angled triangle with sides 36 cm, 36 cm, and 50 cm (14", 14", and 19½") long plus a 1 cm (⅜") seam allowance all around.
Stitch the braid to the longest side of the triangle. Stitch the 2 short sides of the triangle on either side of a corner point of the towel. Turn under the remaining raw edges twice and stitch in place.

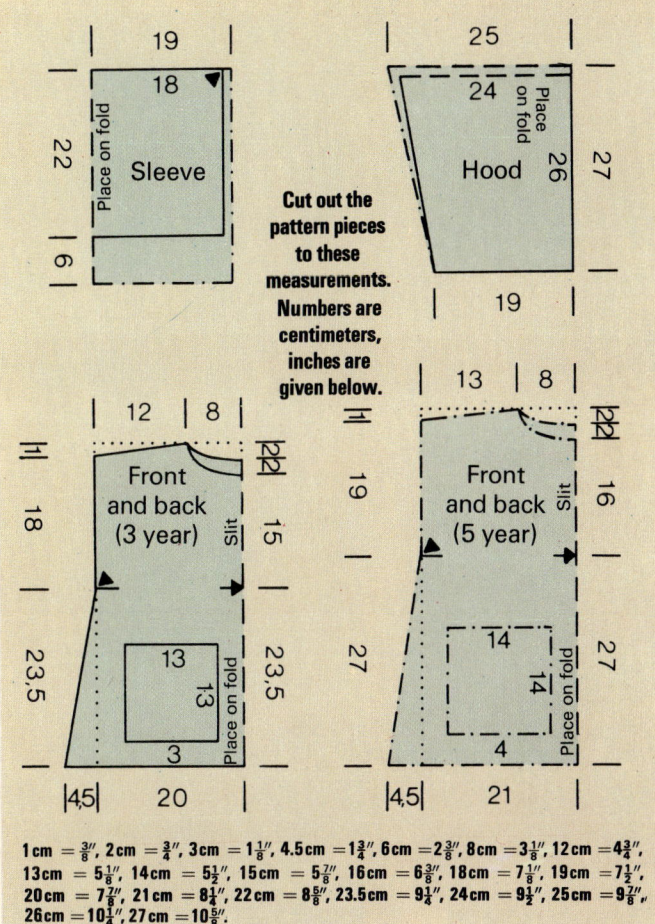

Cut out the pattern pieces to these measurements. Numbers are centimeters, inches are given below.

1cm = ⅜", 2cm = ¾", 3cm = 1⅛", 4.5cm = 1¾", 6cm = 2⅜", 8cm = 3⅛", 12cm = 4¾", 13cm = 5⅛", 14cm = 5½", 15cm = 5⅞", 16cm = 6⅜", 18cm = 7⅛", 19cm = 7½", 20cm = 7⅞", 21cm = 8¼", 22cm = 8⅝", 23.5cm = 9¼", 24cm = 9½", 25cm = 9⅞", 26cm = 10¼", 27cm = 10⅝".

Looped blanket stitch: Insert the needle into the fabric from behind, leaving a loop. Then insert the needle through this loop from behind and pull firmly. In this way, small knots are formed along the top edge.

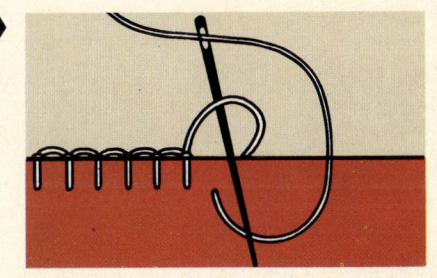

Swing time

Sizes: For 3- and 5-year-olds.

Materials Required:
Felt: 180 cm (72") wide, 0.75 m (⅞ yd) for 3-year-old; 0.85 m (1 yd) for 5-year-old. Soft embroidery cotton: 9 skeins white. Crochet hook. Small amount of white yarn for pompons.

Cutting out: Cut all parts from single fabric without seam allowance, as felt does not fray.

Sewing: Work looped blanket stitch (a variation of the usual method) around all cut edges, 0.75 cm (¼") deep and with the stitches 0.75 cm (¼") apart. Always work from left to right. First, work the upper edges of the pockets, then sew them to the front with blanket stitch. Place the pockets 3.5 cm (1⅜") from the center front (3 years) and 4 cm (1⅝") from center front (5 years). Now embroider all around the other cut edges. Join the shoulder seams by running embroidery thread in and out of the upper loops of the blanket stitches on both parts. Join the side seams in the same way, leaving 8 cm (3") slits at the bottom. Join the side seams. Sew in the sleeves, matching the arrows. Join the back seam of the hood and join the hood to the neck edge. Work 3 pompons as follows: Cut a circle of cardboard 3.5 cm (1⅜") in diameter with a medium-sized hole at the center. The outside edge indicates the size of the finished pompon. Wind the yarn around the circle from the hole to the outside until the hole is completely filled. Then cut the yarn along the outer edge. Wind a length of yarn tightly around the center of the strands. Knot these ends together and leave them hanging down to join to the cord. Shape the pompon into a neat ball.
Crochet one 10 cm (4") long cord of chain stitches for the hood peak and 2 cords each 20 cm (8") long for the neck opening. Fasten the pompons to them. Sew on cords.

Embroidered emblems

Badges, crests and medals

Embroidery

Badges have taken on a new lease of life. The emblems on the badges shown here may not stick strictly to tradition, but they are bright, imaginative, and individual. Decorate jeans, T-shirts, bags, and hats, choosing your own personal symbols, just for fun.

Embroider a badge

This is the brightest way to cheer up your jeans or T-shirts.

737

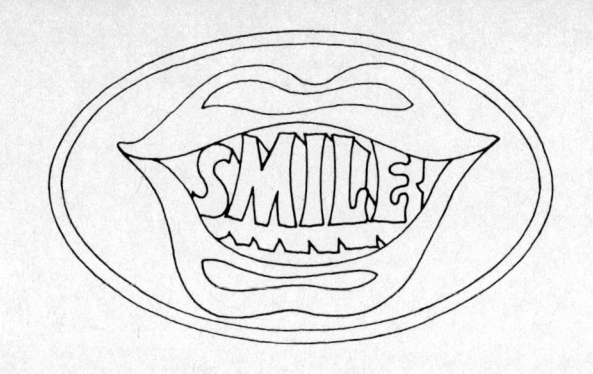

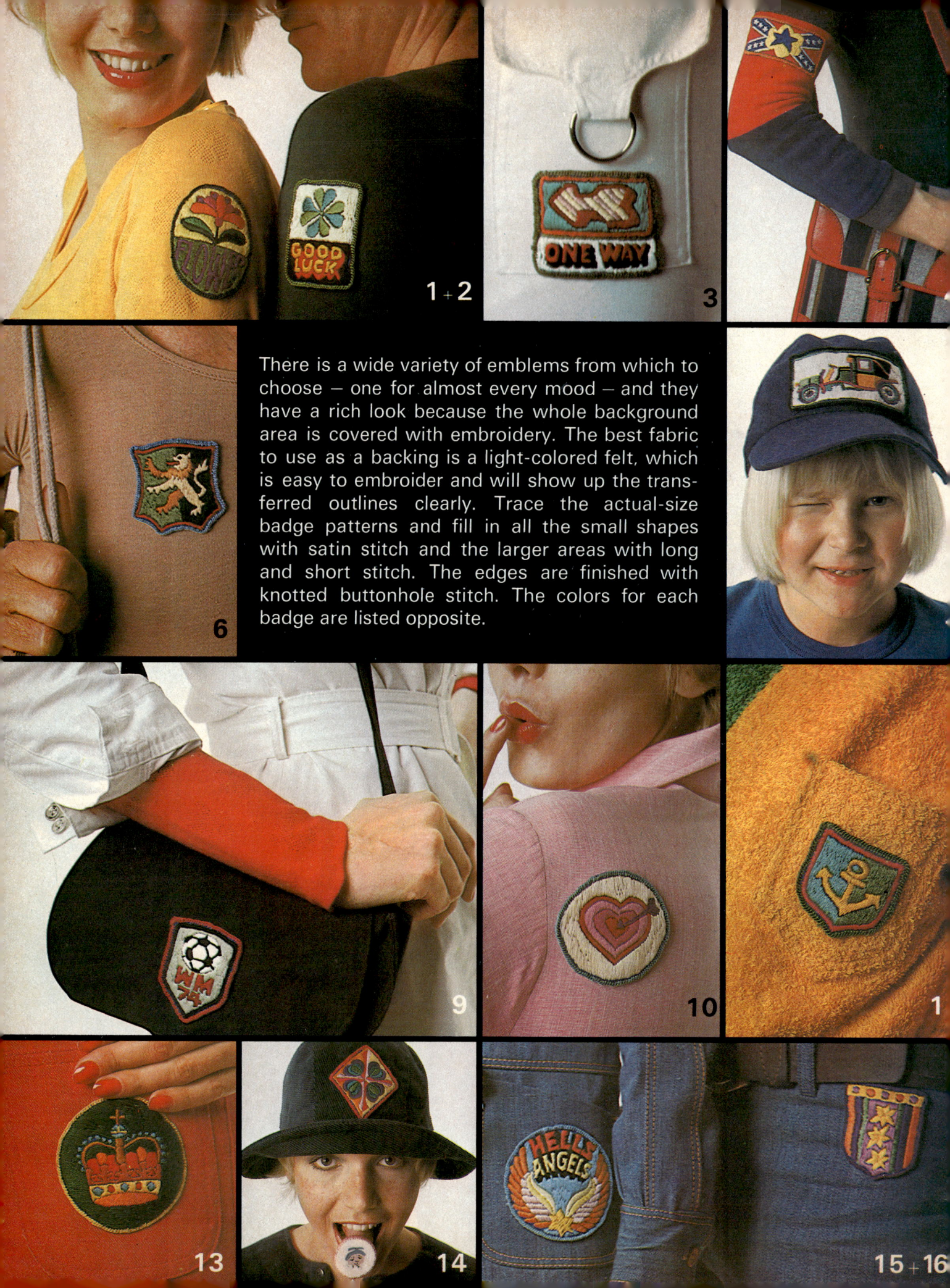

There is a wide variety of emblems from which to choose — one for almost every mood — and they have a rich look because the whole background area is covered with embroidery. The best fabric to use as a backing is a light-colored felt, which is easy to embroider and will show up the transferred outlines clearly. Trace the actual-size badge patterns and fill in all the small shapes with satin stitch and the larger areas with long and short stitch. The edges are finished with knotted buttonhole stitch. The colors for each badge are listed opposite.

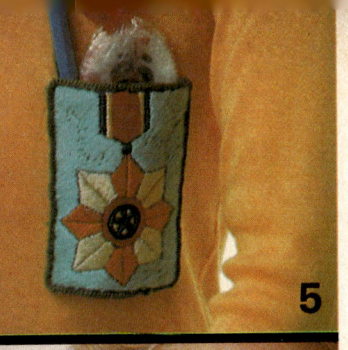

Emblem 1:
Dark green, medium green, lilac, medium yellow, orange, pink, red.

Emblem 2:
Moss green, black, sun yellow, pale yellow, turquoise, bright red.

Emblem 3:
Green, orange, pale blue, red, rose, pale yellow, black, white.

Emblem 4:
Red, dark blue, sun yellow, orange, white.

Emblem 5:
Red, dark blue, pale blue, yellow, gold, pale yellow.

Emblem 6:
Blue, red, pale green, light brown, pale yellow, gold, black.

Emblem 7:
Black, yellow, orange, pink, light blue, mauve, green, brown, white.

Emblem 8:
Rose, bright red, lilac, purple, orange, yellow, cream.

Emblem 9:
White, black, khaki, red.

Emblem 10:
Pale yellow, turquoise, red, dark rose, rose, lilac.

Emblem 11:
Bright red, pale green, turquoise, gold, green.

Emblem 12:
Cream, gold, purple, turquoise.

Emblem 13:
Sun yellow, dark green, turquoise, gold, orange, red.

Emblem 14:
Light red, turquoise, sun yellow, gold, pale rose, mauve, green.

Emblem 15:
Cherry red, medium yellow, black, pale blue, pale yellow, pink, orange, sun yellow.

Emblem 16:
Purple, sun yellow, orange, lilac, green.

Emblem 17:
Pink, green, pale lilac, orange, pale yellow, turquoise, dark green, rose.

How-to

Knotted buttonhole stitch

1 Buttonhole stitch is worked from left to right. There are two methods: for method 1, insert the needle to the required stitch depth. Place the thread around the needle tip and pull the needle through.

2 For method 2, insert the needle and bring it out, but do not pull the thread through completely. Leave a small loop and insert the needle from back to front, then pull the thread through.

3 This is what the work looks like before the thread is pulled tight. The position of the thread is the same in both methods 1 and 2.

4 Always pull the thread taut with the same tension. The row of buttonhole stitching finishes the raw edge and prevents it from fraying.

This idyllic country scene is embroidered in cross-stitch, following the chart overleaf. Surround it with a decorative border, and it's ready to frame and hang up.

Here's a delightful picture for you to embroider. The country scene has all the appeal of 'primitive' art with its bright colors, simple shapes, and bold composition. Give your friends a chance to appreciate your creative talents by framing your picture and hanging it in a prominent position.

*

Size: About 39 cm (15½") wide by 25 cm (10") high.

Materials Required: Stranded embroidery cotton: 1 skein each of the colors listed in the key overleaf. White Hardanger fabric or an even-weave fabric: 24 pairs of threads to 2.5 cm (1"). Heavy cardboard and ordinary straight pins for mounting.

Basic Stitch: The picture is worked in cross-stitch, using 2 strands of stranded cotton. Each square on the chart represents 1 cross-stitch worked over 2 double threads in height and width.

Making the picture

Cut out the fabric, adding 5 cm–10 cm (2"–4") all around the picture area for turning back. Mark the center of the fabric horizontally and vertically with running stitches. Work the picture according to the chart overleaf, beginning at the center. The colors are given on the key; white squares represent fabric which is not embroidered. When the main picture is complete, work the side panels and the border around the edge.

Mounting the picture

Press the embroidery from the wrong side on a well-padded surface. Press lightly so that the stitching will not be flattened.

Stretch the embroidery over the cardboard and place pins into the edges at each corner to hold it in place. Pin the centers of the four sides, but do not push the pins all the way in until the piece has been completely mounted. Continue to pin the edges, dividing and subdividing the spaces between the pins until there is a border of pins around the cardboard 1 cm (⅜") apart. Use a ruler to check that the lines of stitches are straight; adjust the pins if necessary. When the embroidery is in place, drive in all of the pins. Tape the fabric edges at the back or lace them together with long zigzag stitches. Frame the picture as desired.

Worked in cross-stitch

A pastoral scene

741

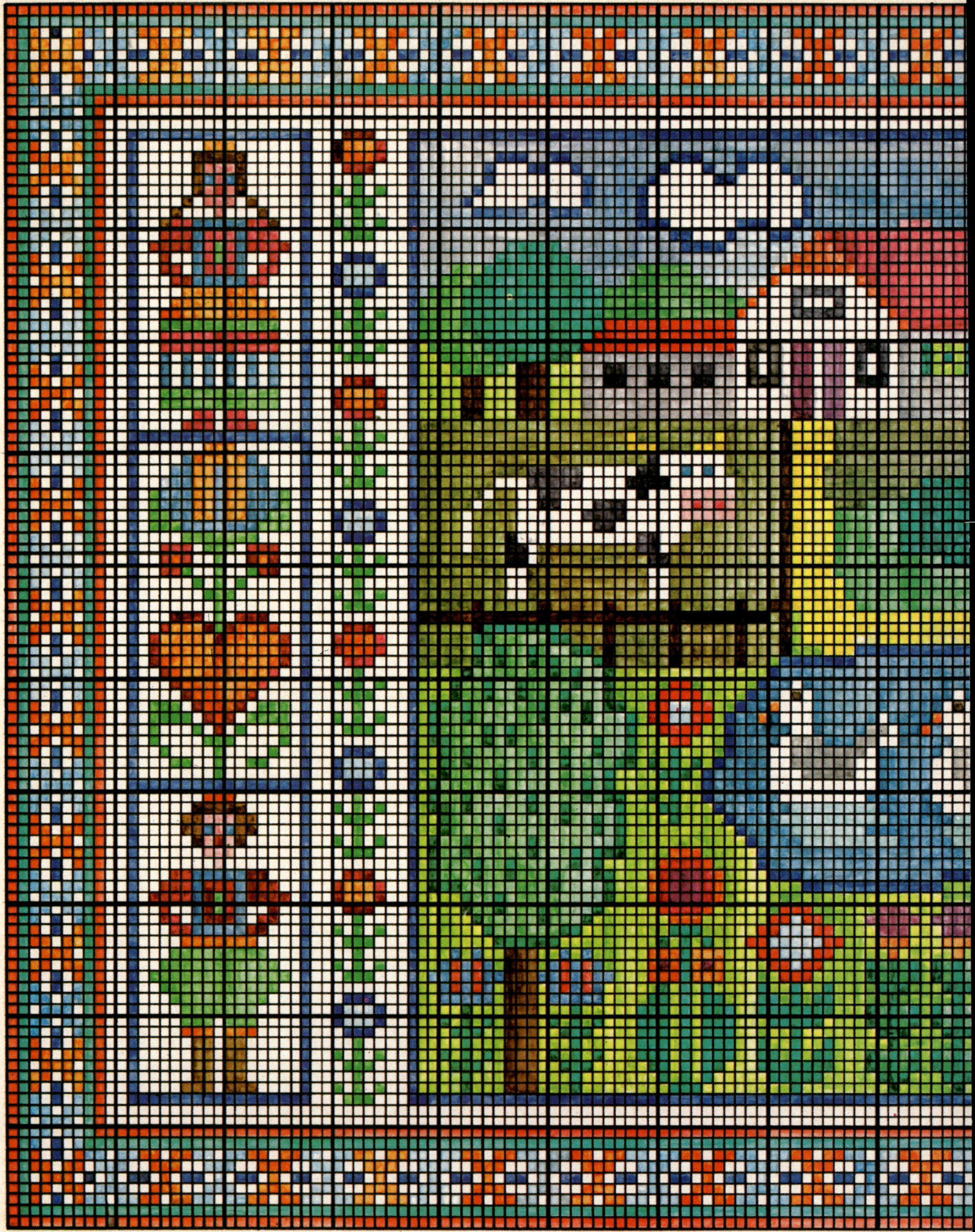

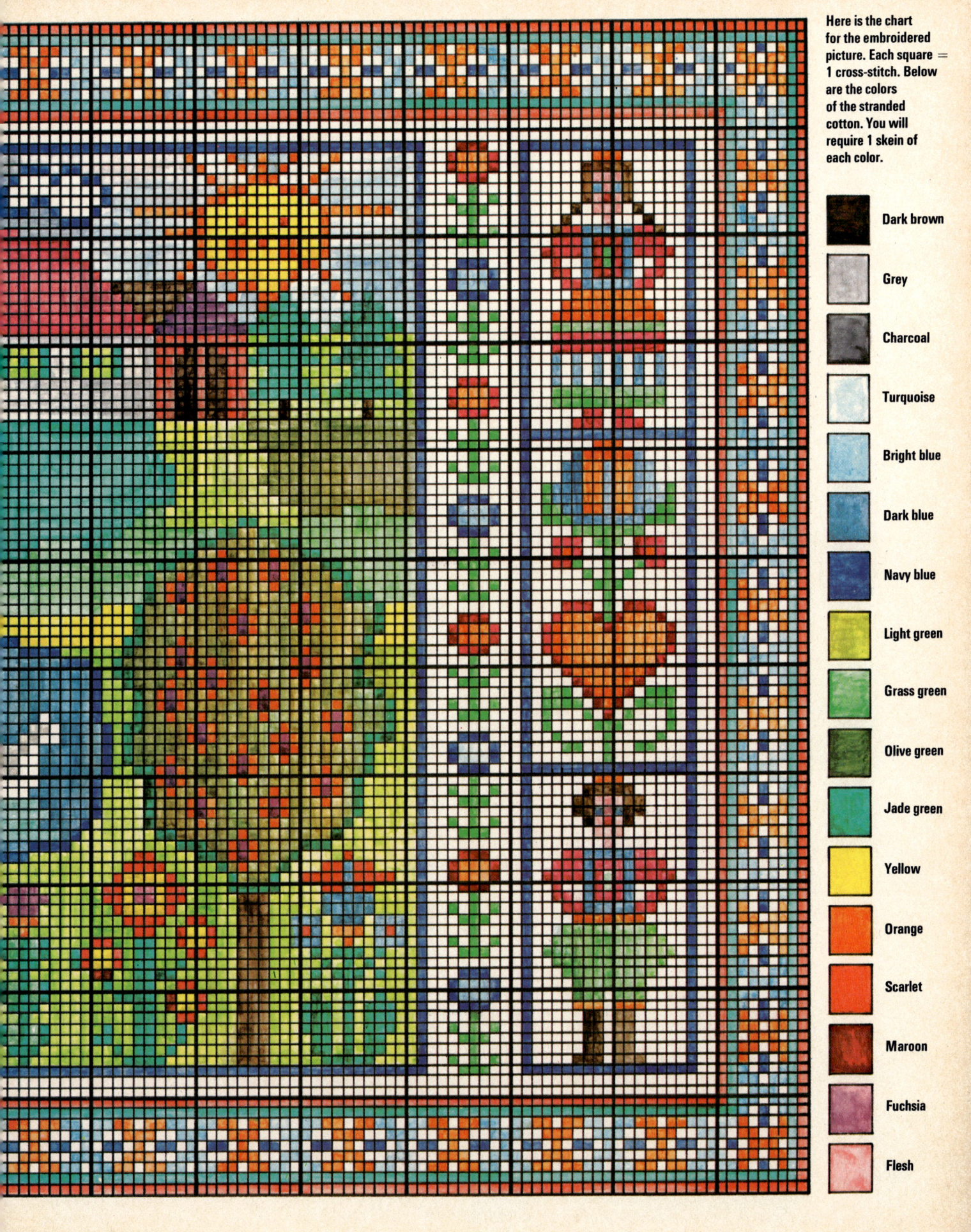

Here is the chart for the embroidered picture. Each square = 1 cross-stitch. Below are the colors of the stranded cotton. You will require 1 skein of each color.

- Dark brown
- Grey
- Charcoal
- Turquoise
- Bright blue
- Dark blue
- Navy blue
- Light green
- Grass green
- Olive green
- Jade green
- Yellow
- Orange
- Scarlet
- Maroon
- Fuchsia
- Flesh

743

How-to

Working cross-stitch over canvas

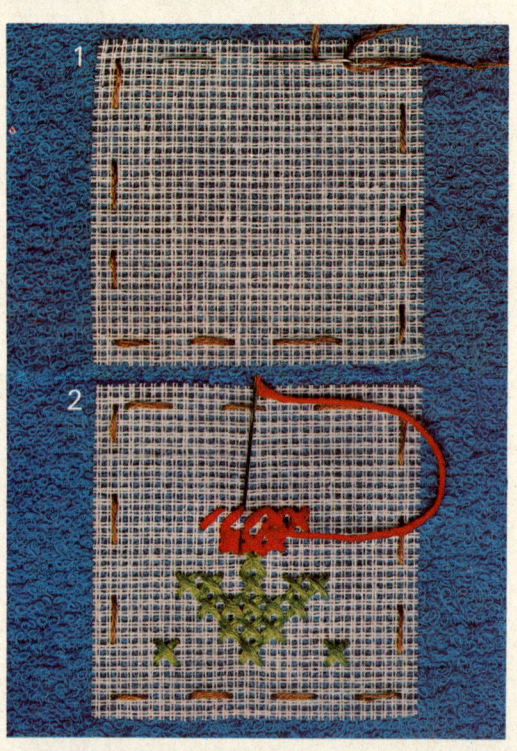

1 First, cut a piece of medium-weave canvas about 1 cm (3/8") larger all around than the desired size of the motif. Baste the canvas to the fabric.

2 Work the cross-stitch tightly over the appropriate number of canvas threads (we worked over 2). Pile fabrics should be worked with all 6 strands, smooth fabrics with divided strands.

3 Take out the basting thread and cut away the canvas close to the motif. Then draw out the horizontal and vertical threads, one by one, leaving the motif on the fabric. Fabrics which are not even weave can be worked in this way.

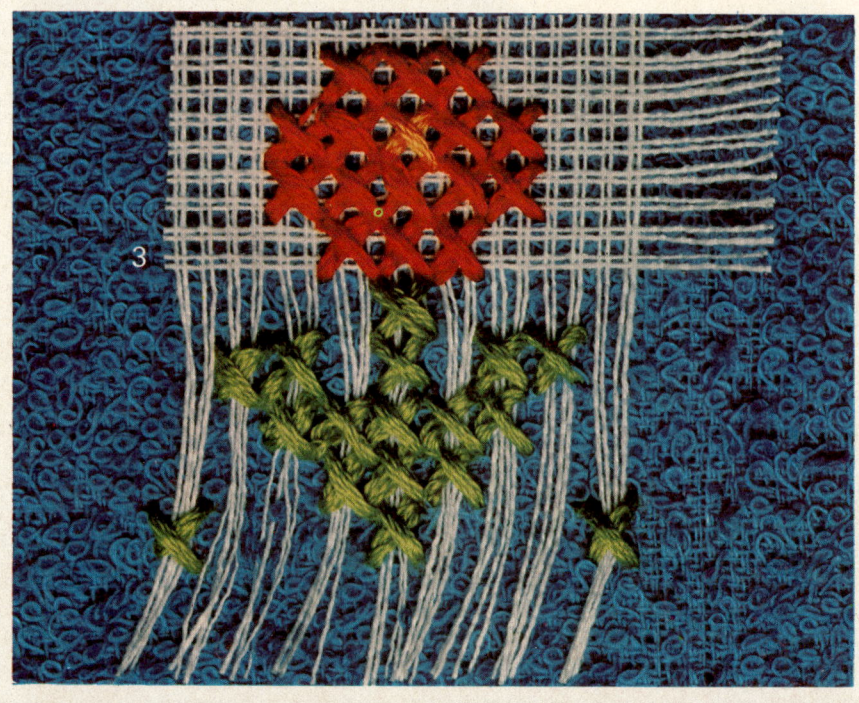

What's your motif?

A pretty cross-stitch motif will brighten up any garment and it's a good way to use up all your odds and ends of embroidery thread. Here is a selection for clothes to suit everyone.

All the motifs shown here are worked in cross-stitch, using stranded embroidery cotton. You can count the number of stitches from the detailed photograph above. Choose colors to suit the color of the background fabric.
The method of working cross-stitch onto fabric

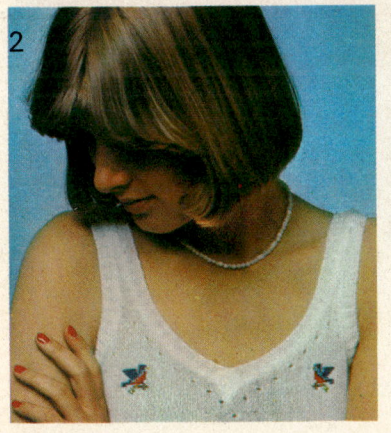

which hasn't got an even weave is shown on the left. This method was used for the dungarees' bib (1) and the baby's bib (3). On the denim fabric, we used 3 strands of stranded cotton, while on the towelling, all 6 strands were used to cover the fabric.
On knitted garments such as the white top (2), work the cross-stitches by counting the knitted stitches.
On this top, we worked one cross-stitch for each knitted stitch, using 3 strands of cotton. The red skirt (4) is made in an even weave fabric onto which the embroidery was worked by counting the threads. We used 3 strands of cotton and worked over 4 threads.

Embroidery

Turn your back on the world

Here's a design with winter sports in mind. These colorful skiers, speeding their way down the back of your jacket, will put you in an active mood even if you are miles from the slopes.

There's no better way of brightening up plain blouses, shirts, or jackets than with some colorful embroidery. Teenagers especially love this form of decoration. Here we give you some inspiration with one winter and one summer design. All the outlines and filled-in areas are worked in chain stitch with undivided embroidery cotton. The designs are given actual size on the trace pattern.

Materials Required:
Embroidery needle. Embroidery hoop (optional). Stranded cotton in the following colors: <u>Winter scene:</u> 1 skein each of white, black, yellow, pale blue, dark blue, violet, brown, green, dark green, burgundy. <u>Summer scene:</u> 1 skein each of white, black, green, dark green, turquoise, cornflower blue, brown, orange, old rose, and dark red.

Working the embroidery
Transfer the chosen motif onto the jacket with dressmaker's carbon paper. Use a light colored paper for a dark fabric and vice versa. To make the embroidery stand out, we worked all the lines in chain stitch with undivided stranded cotton. The larger areas are also filled in with chain stitch. Use the illustrations as a guide to the positioning of the colors.

There's activity of a different kind in this idyllic summer scene which will appeal to the sun worshippers among you. Embroider the design onto a cotton jersey jacket or a denim jacket.

Sports scenes

749

Clown

Peasant Girl

Devil

Make your own puppets and . . .

Come to the show!

If you are ever at a loss to think of an original present for the children, why not make them a set of puppets. They will love making up their own plays and will keep you entertained for hours with stories of adventure and magic.

The puppet parade shown here includes all the old, well-loved fairy-tale characters — the king and queen, the beautiful peasant girl, the wicked witch, an ever-reliable policeman, and many more. They are not as intricate to make as they look — all you need is a little time and patience and lots of remnants of fabrics and trims from your scrap bag. Your imagination does the rest. The puppet heads are made of sawdust and you can make the features as realistic or as grotesque as you like.

Queen

Policeman

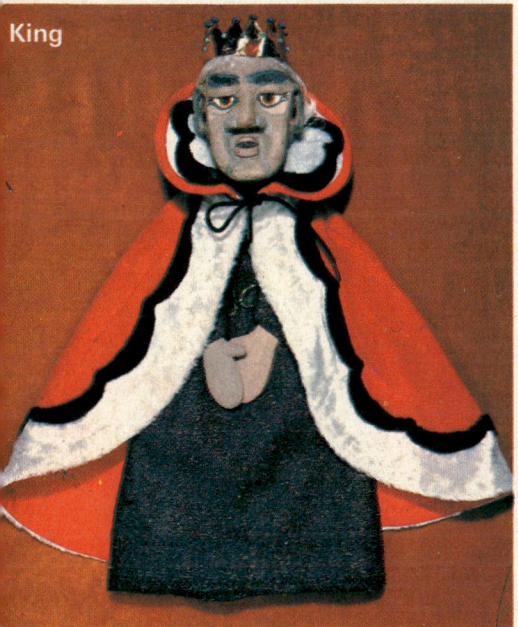

King

Robber

Magician

Witch

The Clown: The most lovable character in the show is the comic clown. We've given him a multi-colored costume trimmed with braid, pompons and a ruff, and a bell which dangles from the end of his cap.

The Queen: Exquisite in gold and lace, the Queen is a very stately figure. She has beautifully curled hair and a layered ruff. Use all the richest trimmings you can find for her dress.

The Policeman: Always ready to come to the rescue, the policeman is smartly dressed in his dark uniform, peaked cap, and white shirt. He carries his gun in a special holster.

The Peasant Girl: She's as demure as ever in her clean white apron and starched collar. Her long blonde braids are made of yarn.

The King: He's a rather serious character, burdened as he is with weighty affairs of state. Give him a suitably regal appearance with a sumptuous, ermine-trimmed cloak.

The Robber: Have fun making him as unkempt as possible, with straggly hair and patched clothes. Don't forget a bag for his swag.

The Devil: One of the villains of any play, he's an impressive sight in red and black with a little touch of green. Give him curved horns and devilish arched black eyebrows.

The Magician: Anything could happen while this character is around. His traditional costume glitters with silver braid and is dotted with symbolic moons and stars. A tall, pointed hat completes the outfit.

The Witch: Another wicked character, the Witch has grotesque features and ugly clothes. To make her even more hideous, paint her face green and add a few warts for good measure.

The method of making the puppets and basic patterns for costumes are overleaf.

Making the costumes

Use remnants for the outfits. Follow our ideas or make up your own.

On this page, you will find actual-size patterns for the basic shapes. The trimmings and accessories, e.g. braid, pockets, belts, ruffs, bags, etc. are left to your imagination. The puppets' dresses all have the same basic shape, but come in two sizes. For the smaller puppets (Queen, Witch, Peasant Girl, Policeman, Robber), Basic Pattern 1 is used; for the larger ones (Clown, Devil, King, Magician), Basic Pattern 2 is used. The sleeve length is indicated for each puppet. The neckline is straight across at the back on all patterns, slightly rounded at the front except for the Clown and Policeman (see pattern). The Devil and King have large capes gathered with ribbon at the neck. The King's cape has a large collar.

Policeman's cap: Cut 2 ovals for cap crown, then from 1 oval, cut away center along curved line A–B. Sew the 2 ovals together at the outer edges. Sew the band along the line A–B. Sew on the peak, matching a and b.

Modelling the heads
Materials Required:

You will need 3 kinds of sawdust – fairly large wood shavings for the egg-sized heads, medium sawdust for the features and neck, and quite fine sawdust for the final details and for correcting unevenness. These can be obtained from your lumber or wood yard. The sawdust is mixed with water and wood glue. To 1 part water and 2 parts glue, add sawdust until you have a firm, fairly dry consistency which can be worked like clay. You will also require basting thread, matches, a file, fine sandpaper, a small screwdriver, a bowl, paint brush, poster paint, glue.

The puppets' hands are cut out in cardboard first; they measure about 4 cm x 2.5 cm ($1\frac{1}{2}$" x 1"). Shape the hands with the fine sawdust mixture. A 3 cm ($1\frac{1}{4}$") wide cardboard ring is stuck on at the base, into which you insert your fingers when using the puppet. The hands are glued into the sleeves.

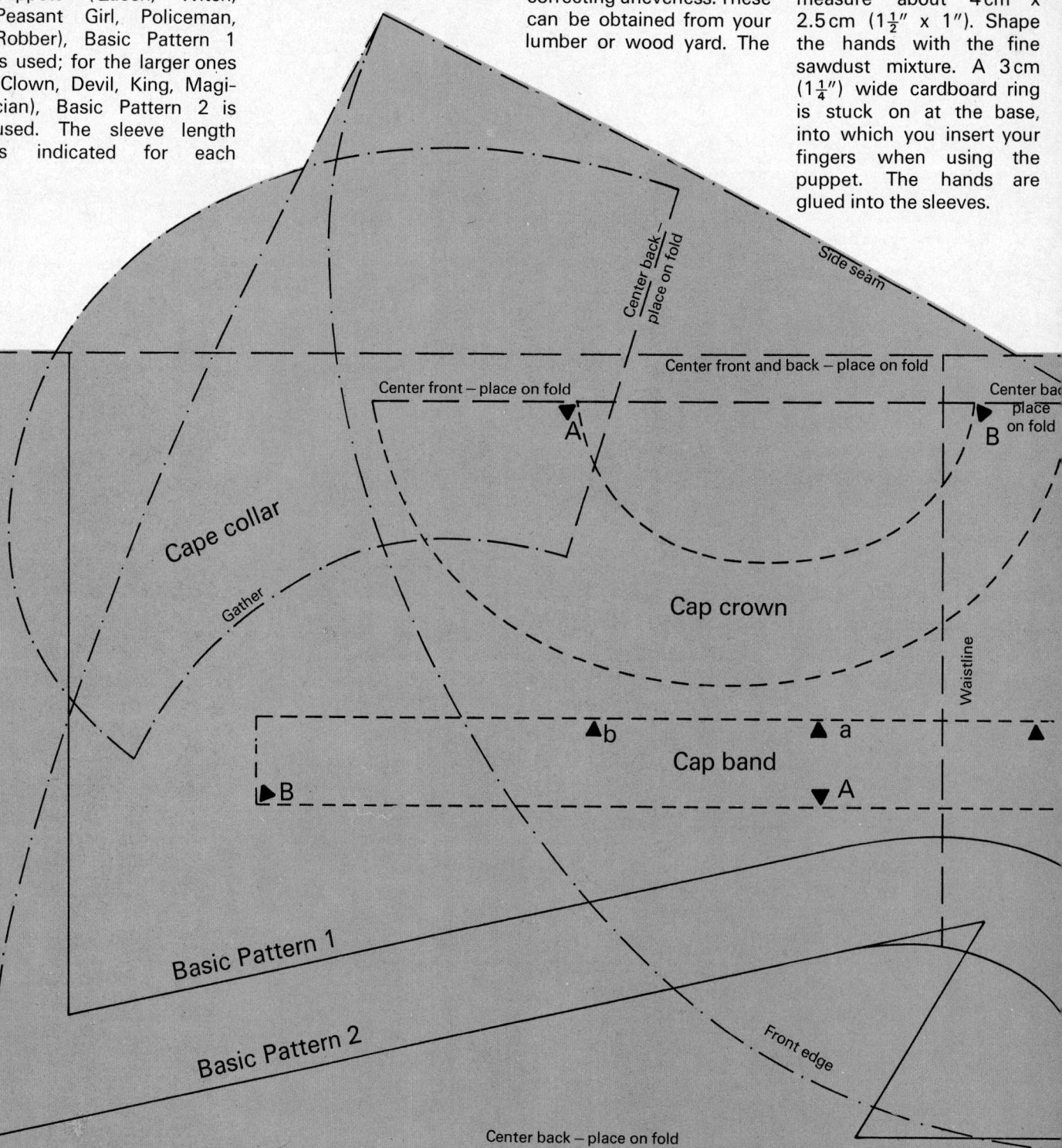

1 Materials. **2** Make an egg-sized coarse sawdust base, wind thread around it; leave to dry overnight.

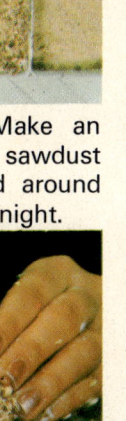

3 Make a finger-sized hole. **4** Build up the neck around the hole in medium sawdust.

5 Shape the large features in medium sawdust, supporting the long ones such as horns with matchsticks.

6 Model the detailed features of the face with fine sawdust.

7 File the head until it is smooth, correcting any unevenness.

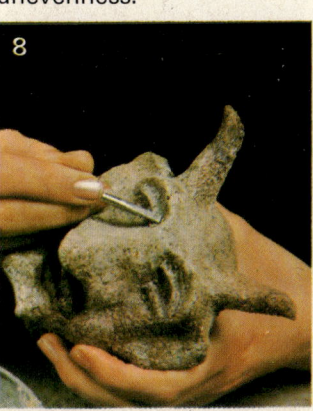

8 Model eyes, lips, wrinkles, warts, etc. with the screwdriver.

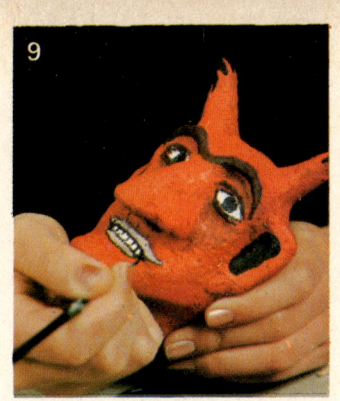

9 Apply the basic face color first. Leave to dry well, then paint the eyes, mouth, ears, eyebrows, etc.

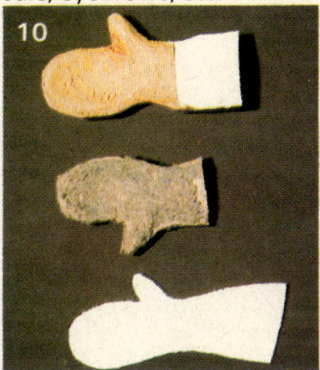

10 Shape fine sawdust over cardboard hands. Add a cardboard cuff.

11 Stitch hair onto a piece of fabric to form a parting. Glue onto head.

12 The peasant girl's braids are made of yarn as shown.

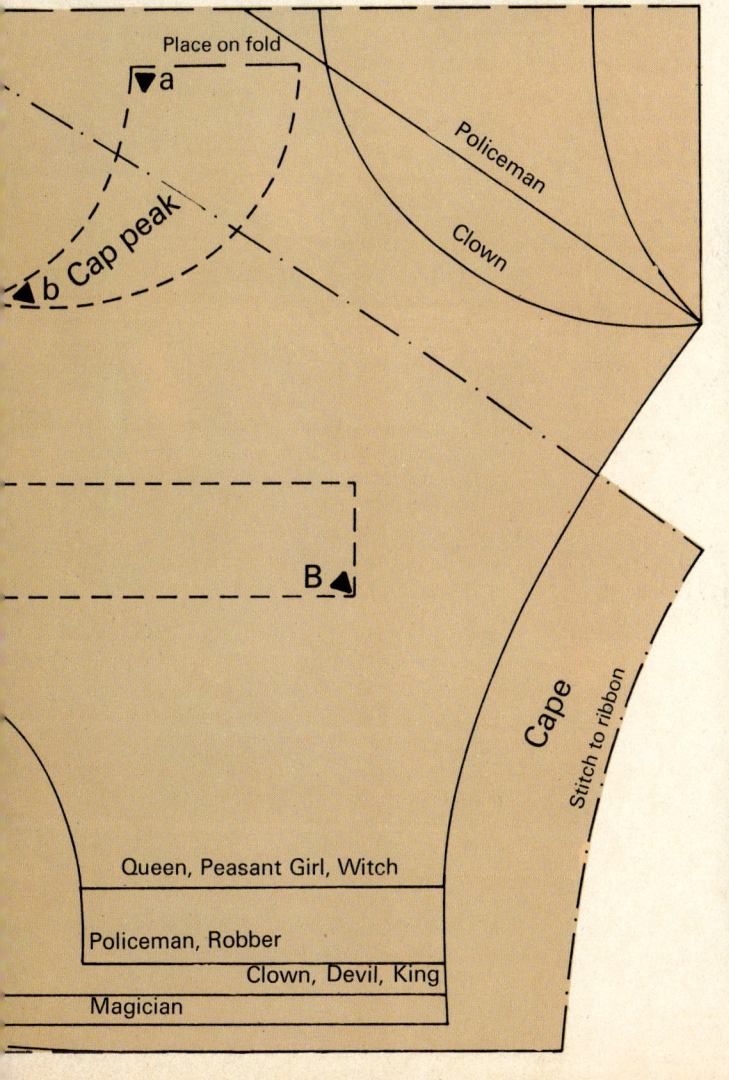

753

Cheap glasses from a department store are gaily painted.

Paint these glasses for your children's birthday parties.

A flower arrangement will fill a corner of your window.

Glassy looks

Painting on glass is an unusual hobby with great potential for budding artists. Begin with our motifs, tracing the outlines from the pattern. As you develop a feel for the materials, try some designs of your own.

The designs are given full size on the pattern.

Materials Required: Enamel paints for glass painting: brown, red, olive, dark blue, white, black, lilac, and yellow. Fine and medium paintbrushes. Adhesive tape.

Painting the glass
Before painting, make sure the glass is free of grease and dust spots. Cut out the desired motif from the trace pattern, leaving about 1 cm ($\frac{3}{8}$") all around the edges. Stick it under the sheet of glass or inside the glasses with adhesive tape. Stir the paint thoroughly.
Now you can begin painting, following the outlines of the pattern. First fill in the larger areas, smoothly and let them dry well (the surface dries in about 4 hours). This is important as the paint runs easily when wet. Then paint in the details such as the features, the flower centers and the outlines with the fine brush.
When the motifs are complete, leave the object to dry. It will take about 3 days to dry completely.
To make a finished edge around square or rectangular pictures, edge the glass with colored tape, catching in rings for hanging. Alternatively, surround with metal channeling and solder on rings for hanging.

Paint this quaint couple for a cottage setting.

756

Painting on glass

Special glass paints are used for these charming motifs which can be applied to tumblers, plaques, or even windows.

Cutting comments

Block printing is a wonderful way to make your own fabric designs. We've printed fabric for a tablecloth and cushions to illustrate the technique. The designs are given opposite. Enlarge them onto graph paper with 0.5 cm ($\frac{1}{4}$") squares. The size of our tablecloth is 128 cm (50$\frac{1}{2}$") square. We printed the edge with the rectangular pattern, the inner area with rows of the three square patterns. The cushion covers are 41 cm (16") square.

Materials Required:
Linoleum. Linoleum cutting set: handle and blades. Rubber roller. Sheet of glass or plastic for inking slab. Fabric. Fabric paints. Methylated spirits for cleaning the printing block and roller. Pieces of wood as a base for the linoleum. Craft knife. Paint brush. White crayon. Pencil. Ruler.
Linoleum: Use the specially prepared blocks available in craft shops or ordinary floor linoleum.
Paint: Use special fabric-printing paints or dyes, available from art and craft shops. They come in a wide range of colors.
Fabric: We used cotton for the tablecloth and cushions. You can, however, print on any closely-woven fabric made of natural fibres. Lino printing is not suitable for roughly-woven fabrics. Fabrics with a lot of sizing or dressing should be washed before use, otherwise the color may be washed out with the fabric finish. Wash the whole length of fabric before you begin and cut out only after printing.

Transferring the design: Tape the design onto the linoleum with dressmaker's carbon paper in between. Trace all the lines with a pencil.

Lift off the paper and cut the linoleum to the proper size with the craft knife. With a white pencil fill in the parts that are to be printed as it is easy to make mistakes when cutting.

Cutting out: Cut around the design outlines with the finest blade — but do not cut into backing.

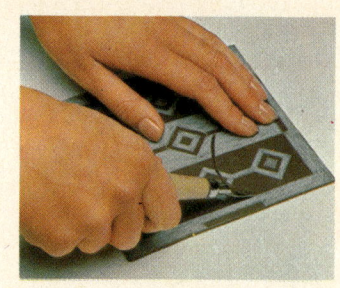

Cut out the areas not to be printed with a blade of the relevant width (never cut toward your other hand!). Correct any unevenness with the fine blade. Now glue the finished piece onto a wooden block, the same size as the linoleum to enable you to see the edges when printing.

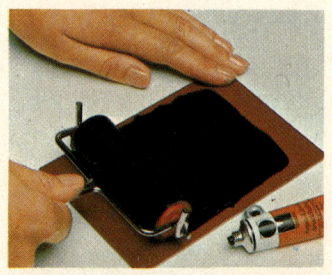

Printing: Squeeze a little paint onto the inking slab. Spread evenly with roller.

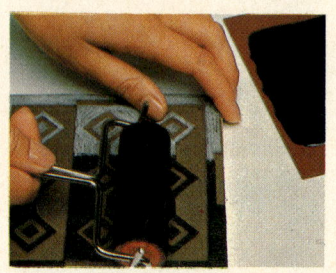

Now roll the paint evenly over the block.

Make a few test prints to make sure the color is not too faint or too strong, then begin the actual printing. The best place is on the floor on a thick layer of newspapers. The paper must lie flat, as every crease will be visible in the print. Place the block flat onto the fabric. To exert a maximum pressure, stand on the block for about 30 seconds, then get off carefully. Alternatively, tap the back of the block all over with a wooden mallet. Roll on more paint and continue to print. Correct any unevenness in the pattern with a paint brush.

The fabric must now be left to dry, for several days if necessary. When the fabric is completely dry, iron it (usually on the reverse side, but check with the paint manufacturer's instructions) with a hot iron. This fixes the color fast to the fabric and the print is then washable.

Finally, cut the fabric out to the correct size. Hem the tablecloth. Sew up 3 sides of the cushion covers and insert zipper in 4th side.

Print each cushion with a different pattern to practice the technique.

The tablecloth has been printed with the square designs in the center and the rectangular pattern as an edging. The cushions have been printed with only one design on each. The paints also come in a range of lovely colors.

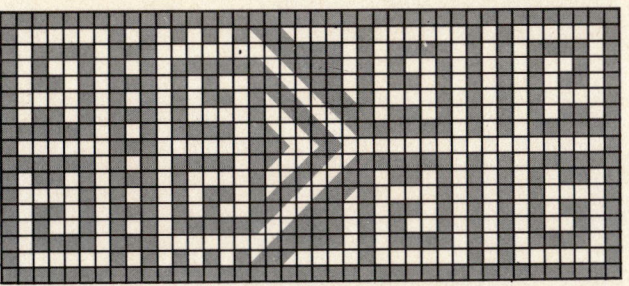

Here are the designs for the linoleum blocks given in a reduced form. Enlarge the motifs onto graph paper with 0.5 cm ($\frac{1}{4}''$) squares to give you the actual-size design. The filled-in squares show the printed area; the white ones are cut out.

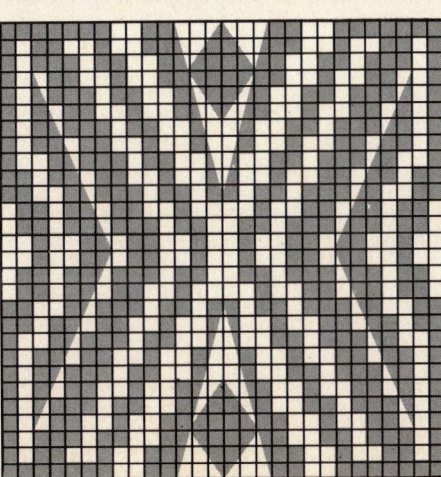

Spring is in the air

Easter decorations should be light-hearted, quick to make and, above all, inexpensive as they will only be used once a year. Our place settings are fun to make, especially for children, and the materials used are all inexpensive. The printed effect of the motifs is achieved by stamping printing colors through a cut-out stencil. If you want a more permanent use for the motifs, try printing on a T-shirt or scarf for yourself, or on sheets or nursery curtains for the children.

Making the place mats

Materials Required: Block of wood with round knob for a handle for printing stamp. Rectangles of foam rubber sheet or felt. Thick elastic bands. Stencil paper or thin cardboard. Permanent fabric printing dyes

1 Trace the motif onto the stencil paper with a pencil and cut out.

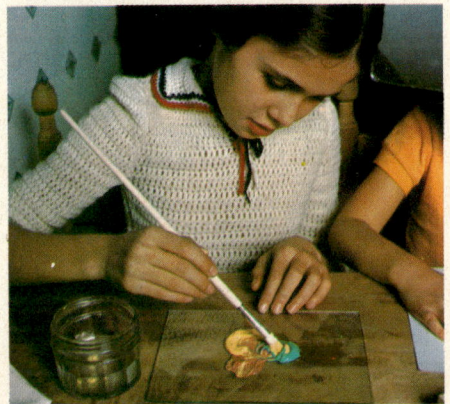

2 Mix enough paint on the glass for all the motifs of one color.

3 Fasten the foam rubber or felt onto the printing block and apply paint.

4 Then place the stencil onto the fabric and "stamp" on the paint.

5 Remove the stencil carefully. Leave paint to dry before continuing to print.

6 The cards are printed in the same way, but you can use poster paints.

7 When using paper, the paint must be quite dry before continuing to print.

8 The end result: a charming and very personal Easter greeting.

in yellow, green, brown, and black. Small, bristle brush. Piece of glass or a plate for mixing the colors. Cotton fabric for the place mats.

Preparing the fabric: Before you begin printing, wash the fabric with soap powder in very hot water. It will then accept the colors more readily and will not shrink any further. For each place mat, cut rectangles of fabric measuring 42 cm x 34 cm (16½" x 13⅜"). Turn the edges in 1 cm (⅜") twice and stitch.

Printing the motifs: The motifs are given as actual-size patterns. Trace the appropriate motif onto the paper,

761

then cut out the shape with a small, pointed pair of scissors or with a craft knife. For the bunny and the grass, you will need only one stencil each; for the chick, you will need two – one for the yellow body and one for the comb, beak, and legs. When printing, make sure that these stencils are positioned exactly.

The actual method of printing is explained with the help of the small step-by-step photographs. To fit the foam rubber sheet or felt to the wooden block, cut it slightly longer than the block on two opposite sides and hold in place with a rubber band. On the place mats, print the grass 3 times along the short sides and 4 times along the long sides, about 1 cm (3/8") from the outer edge. Then print one bunny across each corner and one in the center of each long side. Leave the paint to dry thoroughly after printing, then iron the mats from the wrong side with a hot iron to fix the dyes.

Some other ideas

Another charming idea for using these stencils is to make your own greetings cards. Simply print the motifs onto plain postcards with poster paints and add your message. An egg cup is another novel idea which is easy to reproduce. Print grass and chicks onto a 6 cm x 15 cm (2½" x 6") strip of white cardboard, roll it up, and tape it together.

A homemade card adds a very personal note to an Easter greeting. Why not think up some other motifs such as Easter eggs or flowers?

This photograph shows the motifs positioned on a place mat. They are also most effective on napkins or paper tablecloths.

Our Easter motifs are given here actual size. Trace or transfer the outlines with a pencil and cut out the motifs. For the chick, you will need 2 stencils – 1 for the yellow body and 1 for the brown details. The eye is painted in later.

Index

Afghan crochet
  afghan 688, 690
  cardigan, woman's 682
  hat, woman's 686
  scarf, woman's 686
  stitches
    accentuated color change 689
    afghan knit stitch 685
    afghan stitch 684

Afghan, crocheted 688, 690

Afghan square
  bedspread 694
  Irish rose 698
  joining squares 697
  rug 692

Apron, woman's sewn 719

Baby
  ball, sewn 729
  bed surround, sewn 728
  bib, sewn 730
  changing mat, sewn 729
  covers, sewn 728
  doll, sewn 729
  playsuit
    knitted 672
    sewn 728
  sleeping bag, sewn 730
  towel, sewn 730

Ball, sewn 729

Bed caddy, sewn 727

Bed surround, baby's sewn 728

Bedspread, crocheted 694

Bib, baby's sewn 730

Body measurements chart 649

Bolero, woman's knitted 664

Buttonhole stitch, knotted 739

Cardigan, woman's
  crocheted 682
  knitted 654

Centimeter
  conversion to inches 648
  ruler 649

Changing mat, baby's sewn 729

Children
  dress, knitted 674
  hat, knitted 668
  jacket, sewn 733
  kimono, sewn 716
  playsuit, knitted 674
  pullover, knitted 676, 678, 680
  raincoat, sewn 704
  scarf, knitted 668
  toys 670, 729, 750

Coat, lining Pattern Sheet 22

Collar with a stand 702

Covers, baby's sewn 728

Crafts
  painting on glass 754
  painting on glass pattern 756
  printing
    linoleum block 758
    stencil 760
  puppets 750

Crochet
  afghan 688, 690
  afghan crochet
    accentuated color change 689
    afghan knit stitch 685
    afghan stitch 684
  afghan squares
    bedspread 694
    Irish rose 698
    rug 692
  bedspread 694
  cardigan, woman's 682
  hat, woman's 686
  Irish rose afghan squares 698
  pot holder 699
  scarf, woman's 686
  stitches
    accentuated color change 689
    afghan knit stitch 685
    afghan squares, joining 697
    afghan stitch 684
    Irish rose afghan squares 698
    Tunisian crochet 684

Cross-stitch
  canvas, worked over 744
  motifs 744
  picture 740

Dart, knitted bust 656

Doll
  knitted 670
  sewn 729

Dress, child's knitted 674

Dressmaking—see Sewing

Embroidery
  cross-stitch
    canvas, worked over 744
    motifs 744
    picture 740
  embroidery patterns 736, 748
  patches 734
  sports scenes 746
  stitches
    buttonhole stitch, knotted 739

Fabric
  cutting checked Pattern Sheet 23
  working with coated 706

Glass, painting on 754

Hand puppet, sawdust 750

Hat
  child's knitted 668
  woman's
    crocheted 686
    knitted 660

Illustrated Sewing—see also Sewing

Illustrated Sewing 21 700

Illustrated Sewing 22 704

Illustrated Sewing 23 708

Illustrated Sewing 24 712

Inch
  conversion to centimeters 648
  ruler 648

Irish rose afghan square 698

Jacket
  child's sewn 733
  woman's
    knitted 652
    sewn 700

Kimono, sewn
  child's 716
  man's 716
  woman's 716

Index

Knitting
  bolero, woman's 664
  border, sewing on 656
  bust dart 656
  cardigan, woman's 654
  dress, child's 674
  hat
    child's 668
    woman's 660
  jacket, woman's 653
  playsuit
    baby's 672
    child's 674
  pullover
    child's 676, 678, 680
    woman's 657, 660, 662, 724
  scarf
    child's 668
    woman's 666
  stole, woman's 651
  toys 670
  two colors 659

Lining a coat. Pattern Sheet 22
Linoleum block printing 758
Measurements chart, body 649
Measurements, conversion of 649
Men
  kimono, sewn 716
  shirt, sewn 712
Metric
  conversion 648
  ruler 649
Painting on glass 754
Patches, embroidered 734
Pattern Sheet 21—raincoats, woman's
  adapting for additional sizes
  body measurements chart
  making a raglan sleeve
Pattern Sheet 22—raincoats, child's
  adapting for additional sizes
  body measurements chart
  lining a coat
Pattern Sheet 23—skirts, woman's
  adapting for additional sizes
  body measurements chart
  cutting out checked fabric
Pattern Sheet 24—shirts, man's
  adapting for additional sizes
  body measurements chart
  attaching a double yoke
Picture, cross-stitch 740

Playsuit
  baby's
    knitted 672
    sewn 729
  child's knitted 674
Pleat
  box 711
  pocket in a 710
Pocket
  in a knife pleat 710
  patch 714
Pot holder, crocheted 699
Printing
  linoleum block 758
  stencil 760
Pullover, knitted
  child's 676, 678, 680
  woman's 657, 660, 662, 724
Puppets 750
Raincoat, sewn
  child's 704
  woman's 700
Rug, crocheted 692
Scarf
  child's knitted 668
  woman's
    crocheted 686
    knitted 666
Sewing
  apron, woman's 719
  baby, for 728
  bed caddy 727
  coat, lining a Pattern Sheet 22
  coated fabrics, working with 706
  collar with a stand 702
  jacket
    child's 733
    woman's 700
  kimono
    child's 716
    man's 716
    woman's 716
  pleat, box 711
  pocket
    in a pleat 710
    patch 714
  pullover, woman's 724
  raincoat
    child's 704
    woman's 700
  shirt, man's 712
  shirt sleeve slit 715
  skirt, woman's 708, 722

  sleeve, raglan Pattern Sheet 21
  yoke, double Pattern Sheet 24
  zipper, inserting open-ended 707
Shirt, man's 712
Shirt sleeve slit 715
Sizing, fashion 649
Skirt, woman's
  circle 722
  pleated 708
Sleeping bag, baby's sewn 730
Sleeve
  raglan Pattern Sheet 21
  slit 715
Stencils, printing with 760
Stole, woman's knitted 651
Table linens, printed 758, 760
Towel, baby's sewn 730
Toys
  knitted 670
  sawdust 750
  sewn 729
Two-color knitting 659
Vest—see bolero
Women
  apron, sewn 719
  bolero, knitted 664
  cardigan
    crocheted 682
    knitted 654
  hat
    crocheted 686
    knitted 660
  jacket
    knitted 652
    sewn 700
  kimono, sewn 716
  pullover, knitted 657, 660, 662, 724
  raincoat, sewn 700
  scarf
    crocheted 686
    knitted 666
  skirt, sewn 708, 722
  stole, knitted 651
Yarn, selecting 648
Yoke, double Pattern Sheet 24
Zipper, inserting open-ended 707

Notes

Notes

Notes

Notes